George P. Smoote

The Mississippi

And Other Songs. Second Edition

George P. Smoote

The Mississippi
And Other Songs. Second Edition

ISBN/EAN: 9783337181925

Printed in Europe, USA, Canada, Australia, Japan

Cover: Foto ©Thomas Meinert / pixelio.de

More available books at **www.hansebooks.com**

G. P. SMOOTE.

THE MISSISSIPPI

AND

OTHER SONGS

BY GEORGE P. SMOOTE.

Second Edition.

CHICAGO:
F. J. SCHULTE & COMPANY, PUBLISHERS,
298 DEARBORN STREET.

A TRIBUTE.

THE Hon. George P. Smoote, the author of this volume, was born in Hickman County, in the state of Tennessee, on the 28th day of December, 1828, and died on the 22nd day of April, 1891, at his home in Prescott, in the state of Arkansas, aged 62 years 3 months and 24 days. Having studied law and obtained his license to practice in his native state, he emigrated to the state of Arkansas in October, 1850, first settling in Camden, where he remained two years, and thence in 1852, on the formation of that county, he removed to Columbia County and resided in Magnolia until 1877, when he moved to Prescott, where he died. He was a member of the Constitutional Convention of 1861, and also of the Constitutional Convention of 1874. Otherwise he held no civil office except as special judge of the Circuit and Supreme Courts of the state on several occasions.

The writer of this tribute first became acquainted with Captain Smoote, then on the staff of Major-General John P. McCown of the Confederate army, some time in the year 1862. From that time until his death the close relationship of old soldiers was never strained, by the more selfish contact and rivalries of civil life, during a professional and social intimacy of a quarter of a century. I need scarcely say to those who were acquainted with Colonel Smoote's character, that a more fearless man could hardly have been found in an army whose chivalry and courage have not been excelled in any age of the world. Take it all in all, there was never a temperament better suited to the place he filled as a staff officer of so spirited a division as that which formed the extreme left of the Confederate army at Murfreesboro.

Colonel Smoote possessed a poetic temperament, and this, mixed with a philosophy which was one of his peculiar and marked characteristics, made a unique character—just enough eccentric to be different from all other men, but not enough so to detract one iota from a most finely developed congeniality of spirit.

There were few more accurately and thoroughly educated lawyers in the state than he, and, to add to this, he was, as a politician and advocate, a foeman worthy of the steel of the very best of them. This was remarkable, as the two qualities, or rather qualifications, are so seldom blended in one individual.

I believe I may say he was the hardest hitter, the most tenacious fighter, and the fairest foeman I have ever met at the bar. He was the soul of honor and professional courtesy, but woe betide the unfortunate who mistook this for timidity, or presumed on his courtesy too far. But others will speak of him as a civilian. The only object of this is to pay a tribute to the memory of an old comrade in arms. H. G. BUNN.

MEMOIR.

GEORGE PARKER SMOOTE was born in Hickman County, in the state of Tennessee, on the 28th day of December, 1828. His paternal grandfather, Dr. Charles Smoote, was born near Frederick, in the State of Maryland, about the year 1776, and he there married, in the year 1803, Letitia Tyler. In the year 1815 he emigrated to Hickman County, Tennessee, and, having studied medicine, he became prominent as a physician, and more particularly as a surgeon, and practiced his profession until he was prevented from its continuance by the increasing infirmities of old age. He died in the year 1838.

Edward Williams, the maternal grandfather of George Parker Smoote, was a planter, born near Charleston, South Carolina, about the year 1760. In early life he removed to Tennessee, and became the founder of Williamsport, on Duck River, twelve miles west of Columbia, in Maury County, in that state, which still bears his name, and which continued to be his home until his death, which occurred at that place in 1833. He left behind him a large family of children.

John N. Smoote, the oldest child of the above named Dr. Charles Smoote, was born near Frederick, Maryland, in the year 1804, and emigrated to Tennessee with his father, where he also studied medicine, and continued in practice as a physician until he died, in 1841. He married the youngest daughter of Edward Williams in 1826.

She survived him thirteen years, dying in 1839. Of this union there were three children, of whom the subject of this sketch was the oldest. He attended the academy at Williamsport for several sessions during his boyhood. Afterwards he attended the school of David Reeve Arnold, in Maury County, Tennessee, and was there engaged in the study of Latin and mathematics. In that day Arnold had considerable celebrity as a teacher of those branches of learning; he was regarded as a fine scholar, and as a poet of some merit and distinction.

Having concluded his studies with Arnold, George Parker Smoote, or, as he always wrote his name, George P. Smoote, of whom we have hereafter to speak, began the study of law in the office of Edward Dillahunty, a Circuit Judge in Tennessee, of high professional and social standing, was duly admitted to the bar in that state a few months before attaining his majority in the year 1849, and immediately entered upon the practice of his profession at Centreville, in his native county; but in the year 1850 he removed to Camden, Arkansas, and there remained in the practice of his profession until 1852, when he removed to Magnolia, in this state.

At the beginning of the civil war Mr. Smoote enlisted in the Confederate Army, and remained in that service until the war ended, at first as a lieutenant of artillery, later as an aid-de-camp on the staff of Gen. John P. McCown, until the retirement of that officer in 1863, when he was transferred to the provost marshal's department. He was a brave soldier and an efficient officer, discharging all the duties of his position in that sad and trying period with a fidelity that won the applause of all with whom he was thrown, and forming many warm ties of friendship that were only severed by death. He was, however, in all his tastes and instincts essentially a man of peace; and nothing but a sense of duty, as he understood it, could have called him to the field of arms. No one could possess more courage, physical and moral; but no one possessed a heart more keenly sensitive to the suffering and misery inflicted by war.

At the return of peace Mr. Smoote returned to the practice of law at his home in Magnolia, which was the place of his longest residence in this state. For eleven years that he lived at that place he had for a law partner Hon. B. F. Askew, and for ten years he was in partnership with J. M. Kelso, Esq., in the practice of his profession. Except for a short interval during which he lived at Washington, Arkansas, and the period during the war, he remained at Magnolia until 1877, when he removed to Prescott in this state, where he formed a law partnership with Hon. Thomas C. McRae, the present member of Congress from the Third District; a connection that continued until his death, which took place at his home in Prescott suddenly on the 22nd day of April of the year 1891.

In the year 1868 Mr. Smoote became a member of the Methodist Episcopal Church, and soon afterwards he was licensed to preach the gospel; though he never gave up the practice of the legal profession, and only devoted a part of his time to the ministry. But whenever occasion presented itself he preached from time to time, and acceptably, to the people among whom he lived, for about fifteen years, when, for some reason not stated by him, he desired that his license to preach should not be renewed. Probably the increasing demands made on his time in the legal profession rendered this course imperative. He, however, remained a consistent and active member of the church of his adoption until his death.

Though by long habit wedded to the study and practice of law, Mr. Smoote had a strong predilection for speculative philosophy, and more particularly for theological thought. To him the visible outlines and incidents of life were not sufficient; and beyond them he sought for a deeper meaning. Yet his spirit was in no sense controversial, and he lived in the bonds of charity with men of the most opposite beliefs. He had no Procrustean bed to which he required others to conform; but adhered with equal devotion and modesty to the creed that he had espoused. A man of much reading and reflection, his standard of thought was that of the age in which he lived, whose larger toleration was prized by him as a triumph of the religion that he professed.

As a jurist Mr. Smoote stood high in his profession. His studies had been long and laborious, and he brought to the solution of the arduous difficulties of the law a sound, disciplined and discriminating mind. As a practitioner he was zealous, earnest and persuasive; ready for all the vicissitudes of legal warfare. By these qualities and by an innate honesty in the presentation of his views, whether of law or fact, and his undeviating courtesy to others, he won for himself, and maintained until the end, the respect and friendship of the bench and bar, and the confidence of those by whom his services were retained in an extensive practice. These stood very near to him in every-day intercourse; but there were others that stood still closer to him; for he was a man deeply attached to home and family; and it was there that as a father and husband he appeared to most advantage. Loving, tender, patient, considerate, indulgent, he brightened and charmed the circle of his household, and received an equal return for the disinterested and unchanging affection which he always displayed. He was twice married, first to Mrs. Sarah A. Mullins, and, after her death, to Mrs. Julia Goode Mathews, who, with five children by his first wife, still survives him.

Mr. Smoote was highly esteemed by his neighbors and the people who knew him best and longest. He was not a timeserver, and had none of the arts by which official position is attained; but he was frequently assured of the public confidence and respect that his virtues commanded.

He was a member of the State Constitutional Conventions held in 1861 and in 1874, being in both cases the delegate of Columbia County; and during that long interval, and until he died, he preserved the trust and good opinion of the people whom he strove to serve.

What is here said ought not to be laid to the account of that spirit of eulogy which is common when we come to speak of the dead who shall nevermore be moved by praise or blame, and whose virtues, real or assumed, no longer give offense to the living.

If the desires of the deceased, who was a real friend of truth, and who hated all falsehood and exaggeration, were now fulfilled, nothing like extravagant commendation would be spoken or written of him; but rather, like the dying Moor, he would have said:

"Speak of me as I am; nothing extenuate,
Nor set down aught in malice."

Outside of song and romance, and obituary notices, which often borrow the hues of both, the perfect man has no place on earth; but fortunately love, and friendship, and bereavement, and mourning require no such impossible aliment; and they continue to exist without even the help of that charity that covers a multitude of sins.

The philosopher Plato has rescued from oblivion some lines from the poet Simonides expressive of a thought that may be applied alike to the living and the dead.

"I do not hope," he says, "to find a perfectly

blameless man among those who partake of the fruits of the broad-bosomed earth, and when I have found him to tell you of him; in this sense I praise no man. But he who is moderately good, and does no evil, is good for me, who voluntarily love and approve every one who does no evil; though there are others whom I also praise and love unwillingly.''

No man could be freer from conscious evil than Mr. Smoote. It is not probable that he left any enemies. If such there were, they would dwell rather upon foibles than upon any serious faults or deformity of temperament or character. Fairness and justice toward all, frankness and sincerity in all his intercourse were with him fundamental rules of conduct. A man of very strong and decided convictions, he was charitable and kindly disposed towards all men, and deserved the commendation of the angel that "wrote in a book of gold;" for he was one "that loved his fellow men." He was not goaded by ambition, or corroded by envy. His days were given to honest toil, his objects were worthy, and he found the chief pleasure of life in the intimate association of his family and friends, and in a conscience void of offense. In some respects he might have been regarded as eccentric; but never in an offensive way. He was not given to malice, or self-seeking, or the spirit of detraction that underrates the merits of others.

Naturally of a devout turn of mind, he exemplified in his life and conduct his strong faith in the Christian religion, which was to him in the place of ultimate facts not otherwise cognizable here. Under its guidance, and with the aid of a temperament naturally philosophic and free from extremes, he fought the battle of life, and, like all men, sometimes unprevailing; but with steadfast courage and confidence, patience, hope and resignation even unto the end.

The labors of the forum and of the pulpit are in their nature for the most part transitory. Stored only in the perishing memory of men, they are soon forgotten. Spoken discourse soon passes away, but the written words remain.

Mr. Smoote in his life-time wrote various fugitive pieces of poetry that from time to time appeared in newspapers and other publications of that kind. Of all the things that he did they were probably by him the least regarded as possessing any lasting worth; it must not be inferred from this publication that the author looked upon these productions with any sentiment of vanity or self-applause, for he had neither the poet's sensitiveness nor the poet's pride. Unpretending in his manner of life and character, he did not overrate their value, but judged them with a degree of impartiality that might well disarm unfriendly criticism. Indeed, he rarely alluded to them, and they probably occupied but little of his thoughts. They were no doubt regarded by him as mere ephemeral expressions of passing moods of thought, as imperfect manifestations of poetic feeling, not worthy to challenge the serious attention of the general reader, who is usually quick to condemn any work of that kind which does not display that high order of excellency which is beyond the critic's reach. It was well known to him that the poet is born, not made; that the poetic faculty is the rarest of endowments, insomuch that of the countless millions of our race that have inhabited the world the really great poets of all times and countries can easily be counted on one's fingers; and that even of these it must be said that the most of their productions fall far below the high standard to which they have sometimes attained, and upon which their fame substantially rests. He was far from presuming to rival these great sons of genius, who must ever dwell far apart, each one in a sphere of his own, destined, alas,

"To learn in suffering what they teach in song."

He knew also well that many a votary of the muses who for a time achieves popularity, capturing the public favor by beauties or fancies that seem to be new, soon falls into disregard, and is speedily overtaken by darkness and oblivion, overpowered in the lists where mediocrity, or anything less than the absolute supremacy of genius, is doomed. The limitations of power which at an early hour come home to the consciousness of most men were not unfelt or unappreciated by him; and it was not in his character to attach any undue importance to the thoughts that he had committed to the form of verse. There is, however, nothing in them of which he could be ashamed, and nothing to excite regret for wasted time, or talents misapplied. Happy is the man that leaves behind him no worse legacy.

Since the death of Mr. Smoote, his family and immediate friends have thought it permissible to gather together with loving hands the poems written by him at various times, though not unmindful of the fact that they are in many instances but unfinished sketches, lacking the author's final touch, satisfied that in any event they will, in the minds of many who knew him, be received as a cherished memorial of ties that are broken. If it may be urged that these poetic effusions fall below the exalted rank that commands the applause of mankind, it may still be true that they may have their reason for being, though in an humbler and less conspicuous place; for to us ordinary mortals there comes a time when we grow weary of the exacting company of the throned gods of Olympus, whose ardent and strenuous discourse taxes every faculty of mind and heart—those moments in which a true poet, though not of the greatest, has said:

"Come, read to me some poem,
　Some simple and heartfelt lay,
That shall soothe this restless feeling,
　And banish the thoughts of day.

"Not from the grand old masters,
　Not from the bards sublime,
Whose distant footsteps echo
　Through the corridors of time.

"For, like strains of martial music,
　　Their mighty thoughts suggest
Life's endless toil and endeavor;
　　And to-night I long for rest.

"Read from some humbler poet,
　　Whose song gushed from his heart,
As showers from the clouds of summer,
　　Or tears from the eyelids start;

"Who through long days of labor,
　　And nights devoid of ease,
Still heard in his soul the music
　　Of wonderful melodies."

LITTLE ROCK, November 10, 1891.

DEDICATION.

TO MY WIFE.

Dear Julia, unto you I dedicate
This book, unknowing what may be its fate.
Whatever it may seem to others, we
Its making have enjoyed and loved to see
Its lines extend and grow, until at last
'Twas finished and the happy work was passed.
The critic may not find it worth his praise;
Nor does it seek to rival those grand lays
Whose noble music nations love to hear.
Yet you and I, with trembling hope and fear,
Its pages open to the eye and ear
Of every one who has the wish to know
The sentiments and thoughts its verses show.
But, dear, it may not blossom into fame—
It may not wreathe the laurel round my name;
The world may think not of it — it may lie
Unread, uncared for, and, unnoticed, die.
But this we have to risk. What you and I
As fine, and strong, and beautiful may deem,
To other minds as foolishness may seem.
The realm where high Imagination dwells,
And lofty Thought its fervid current wells,
Cannot be reached by ordinary men;
It may be far above my mental ken.

DEDICATION.

But we are not prepared to judge of this.
You would at once decide it with a kiss,
Asserting that the verdict should be mine,
And that my songs are more than half divine;
And I, in loving vanity, would own
That better judge than you was never known.
Fond love can seldom rightly criticise,
Because it always sees with partial eyes.
Therefore, my labor must in patience wait,
And we must willingly accept its fate.
If it commended be, we will rejoice,
Together gladly listening to the voice
Of fame; but if neglect shall darkly gloom
Our hopes, we will in peace abide the doom.
But we have had a sweet and soothing joy,
Which destiny itself cannot destroy,
In reading o'er the songs we now send out
Upon their way to meet the world in doubt.
With what delight we have their merits tried,
In happy converse by our fireside,
Where it was passing sweet to me to hear
The loving words of praise from lips so dear!
Oh! not for all the stars in glory's skies
Would I exchange the light that filled your eyes,
While thus we sat conversing many times,
With earnest, hopeful words about my rhymes,
And hence, dear wife, I deem it not unmeet
To bring my songs and lay them at your feet,
So that with mine I may unite your name,
If they shall bring to me a living fame.

SONGS OF THE MISSISSIPPI.

I.

PRELUDE.

We all love rivers.   E'en the little rills
That gurgle down the valleys round our homes
Live ever in our hearts and memories;
And at all times we feel a joyous swell
Within our souls, and coursing all our veins,
When any flowing river meets the eye
And so I love all streams, but unto thee,
O mighty Mississippi! goes my heart
Before all other rivers of the earth.
I love thee all the more because thy waves
Do flow between the shores of Arkansas,
Where I have lived and loved for forty years,
And those of my own native Tennessee.
And I have hoped to see thy name embalmed
In glowing song immortal as thyself;
And I have listened for those harps renowned,
Which tune the glories of this land of ours,
To sound abroad thy praises and thy fame.
But they are silent; and with trembling hand,
And awed, I now essay the great attempt.
   O ye who sang the heathen gods of old,
In strains that have outlived their fallen shrines—
O bards whose tuneful notes are heard
Above the roar of earth's discordant storms,
Despise not ye, nor scorn my daring lyre,
Though by a village hand 'tis tuned and strung!
If ye do still look on these scenes below,
With any deep regard, or interest take
In mortal songs, which once your glory were,

And can a child of earth inspire with thought,
Oh! fill me now with that celestial fire
Which still along your lofty numbers burns!
It is no mean ambition bids me sing,
To win the shallow praise that lives an hour:
It is the wish to stir, in every soul,
The same abiding love that fills my own,
And utter those emotions which within
My swelling bosom rise when I behold
The Mississippi's waters sweeping by!

II.
BEFORE THE DISCOVERY.

Forth rolled the Mississippi's waves at first,
In stately power, never more to cease
Until eternal night shall close around
The fading scenes of earth; but who can tell
His history for five thousand years and more;
Ages of darkness, pre-historic gloom, [eyes,
Where knowledge folds its wings and shuts its
And dreams uncertain and fantastic dreams.

Age after age thus slowly passed away,
And still no mighty monuments of thought,
Nor marks of empire, well defined, were found
Within the Mississippi's realm of vales.
Through all that waste of time, the eye beholds
Unbroken wilds where beasts ferocious prowl,
Where crested, hissing snakes are gliding by,
Where homeless, roving, savage red men hide,
Where sunlight falls in melancholy streams,
And storms in fury sometimes sweep along —
But not one conquest of the human mind!

Age after age thus slowly passed away,
And still the Mississippi waited for
The coming hand of civilizing Art.
The Indian roved along his winding shores,
Not dreaming once of richly laden fleets,
Nor prairies waving far with corn and wheat,
Nor cotton fields wide spread beneath the sun,
Nor cities, railroads, temples, forums, schools,
Nor of the milk-white banner of the cross,
Borne onward by the inherent moral force
Of love and wisdom in the words of Christ.

Age after age thus slowly passed away,
And still the Mississippi spurned the bark
Canoe, as though no weaker, meaner power
Than some great triumph of the human mind,
Evoking nature's elements of death,
And training them to meet the wants of life,
Was ever destined to control his might.

Age after age thus slowly passed away,
And o'er the Mississippi's valley far,
Still lonesome, gloomy, ancient Solitude
Did brood, with silent, sombre wings out-spread,
Like some vast spirit into slumber lulled
By all the music of that mighty river!

Age after age thus slowly passed away,
And still the Mississippi onward poured [sublime!
His rolling course, through boundless wastes
The stars looked nightly on his lonely flow,
And all alone the dreaming eagle sat,
In silence listening to his rushing waves,
As though their voices had prophetic tones,
That spake to him of empire yet to come,
When from the blue empyrean sky those stars

Should on their chosen banner fall, and he
Should sit triumphant in its blazing folds!
    Meanwhile, the mighty purposes of God
Were slowly opening to the eye of man.
Through all the movements of the ages past,
The eastern half of this old world had felt
The throes of manhood struggling with itself,
For conquest over selfishness and wrong.
Much had been learned; great truths had sprung
    to light;
And conflicts had, for human rights, been fought
By men who did not fear to die for them:
But there the Truth its climax could not reach,
For old Oppression, strong with gathered might,
Was firmly seated on the thrones of earth,
And there were hoary Errors, unhealed wounds,
And hardened falsehoods, consecrated long
By time; and narrow creeds for human faith,
Enforced by fierce, despotic, cruel power,
Confining all that God had taught to man,
And marring all the sacred lines of Truth!
But in that very strife of ages past,
Which seemed to fetter human hope to earth,
The thoughts on which the world's salvation
    hangs,
Evolving slowly, struggled into life;
And man, at last, had fully learned to know
And feel the worth of all essential things,
In Morals and in State. The question was,
How should that hard-won lore have scope and
    strength,
How overcome opposing power and break
The fetters binding down the arms of Truth,

And give the Nations their high jubilee?
For bitter misrule, want and woe had made
The Truth itself a danger in the hands
Of those who had endured and suffered most,
And drove them often into bad extremes.
'Tis true that isolated men could stand,
And sing hosannas at the martyr's stake,
And there, for God or Country, bravely die;
Or strike Oppression on the battle-field,
Or speak for human rights in senate halls,
In spite of tyrant's power and headsman's axe.
But of the Nations, what? Must all the good—
Must all the gems of light, which hope and faith
And labor long had scattered o'er the earth,
Be lost, or to no greater purpose reach
Than just to show a hero here and there?
The great unanswered want of man was, then,
Another new and uncorrupted world,
Where stagnant wrong was not in all the air,
And all that struggling thought had dearly won
Of good could take a fresh and hardy growth.
And so the grace of God Columbus raised,
And made him Moses of the unknown seas,
And filled his heart with that abiding faith
Which fears not pathless oceans in its way,
And conquers dangers, deserts, mountains, all,
Before the timid skeptic dares to move!
He found that other world, and in the West
A new career was opened wide for man,
And Mississippi's shores were marked and set
For freedom's refuge and the right of thought.

 The Stern and Brave, who would not have their
  minds

Confined by any narrow creed of earth,
Who dared to think in Superstition's face,
And scorned the fetters of old Tyranny,
Came landing fast upon the shores of James,
By Plymouth Rock, on Carolina's sands,
And thence, with all their glowing human hopes,
Commenced their long and weary march to thee,
O giant river of the western world!
And so we learn why for five thousand years
And more, reserved by Wisdom Infinite,
Thy waters flowed in solitary gloom.

III.

DISCOVERY OF THE MISSISSIPPI BY DE SOTO.

    Far southward stands a bold and lofty bluff,
Upon the Mississippi's eastern shore.
To-day, a splendid city crowns its crest.
There Chinca, savage village, struggled once,
And there the savage hunters of the wild
Brought in their spoil, from all the forest round,
And there a savage chieftain held his court,
And there Cacuique and Sachem, old and wise,
And tattooed warriors, fierce and grim, did meet
That chief, in council high and grave debate
And there, in savage glee, the green-corn dance
Was held, when July's moon was bright in
      heaven.
Imagination wings its backward flight

To Chinca's bluff, three hundred years ago
And more, and stands, intent, beside that Chief,
With all his painted warriors round him there,
Upon the margin of their sacred river,
And, through primeval forests gazing, sees
De Soto's waving plume and warlike form
Approaching, with his weather-beaten men —
Not thinking once how great that march would
      make
That day, throughout the years of coming time,
Until they there beheld, in grandeur spread,
The mighty Mississippi pouring south!
It was a scene worth more than all their toils,
And every danger passed on that long march.
And there De Soto and his weary band
Might well have sent up, reaching to the sky,
A shout of triumph at the thrilling sight!
But oh! it wrings and pains my heart to tell
That low, ignoble love of gems and gold
Inspired the enterprise which wrought this end.
I deeply mourn that such a brave event
Should e'er have been the work of such a chance!

    Had any purpose pure, ambition high,
Impelled those wanderers when they reached thy
      shore,
O swift and broad and deep and noble river,
Then would the Muse, exulting, sing their praise,
But as she stands enraptured by thy waves
When first they grandly rolled before the eyes
Of men from far-off Europe's Christian land.
Her joy is all for thee. For them she weeps,
And for De Soto most. He had a soul

Well worthy of this deed for its own sake.
But Mammon, whose destroying shadow falls
Upon so much that otherwise were great,
Or pure, or beautiful, did spoil his fame,
And then his search and grasp and hope elude!
Small praise is due him for the great result
Which did from his ignoble purpose spring.
He sought not glory nor the good of man;
His heart was filled with dreams of diamond
    fields,
And far-off valleys, bright with golden sand!
So moved not, nor rejoicing, with his heart
Still on some shining Eldorado set,
That foaming current only seemed to him
A wide impediment of liquid gloom,
Obstructing further search for sordid pelf.
And so De Soto and his men, to cross
That river, labored hard by day and night.
They brought forth hammer, axe and saw, and
    loud
Within the grand old forest rang their blows,
Arousing echoes never heard before
Along their shaded, gloomy, ancient aisles.
Old oaks and pines and poplars thundered down,
With far-resounding crash! and their huge trunks
Were hewed and sawed and worked, until there
    lay
Eight well-formed keels upon the river's shore.
Then rose the slender masts. Then came the oars,
And then, with strain and shout, they glided off,
The first rude fleet that Japhet's sons did launch
Upon that river's yielding breast. 'Tis true
'Twas all unworthy of such fame as that;

But grand it must have seemed to savage men,
Whose rocking, light flotilla of canoes
By hundreds hovered far around, in fear.
At length, the winds which down that vista sweep
(That mighty vista through the forest torn,
From far Itasca to the stormy Gulf)
Did for the first time fill the spreading sails
Above the current of that mighty stream,
And bore those strangers to the farther shore.

  It had been better for those wanderers then,
It had been better for their leader's fame,
If their unholy quest had ended there.
A splendid consummation, all unsought,
Would then have crowned their weary march, and thrown
Concealing glory o'er the low intent
Which had their only inspiration been.
But that intent still drew them fiercely on,
Until the Rocky Mountains barred their way,
With pathless wilds, and lofty peaks and crags,
And deep ravines, and everlasting snow!
Beyond those mountains glowed the mines they sought,
Denied to them and all their toils, by fate.
Repelled by nature's frowning sentinels,
With hopeless, saddened hearts and drooping strength,
They turned in sorrow from their fruitless search,
And marched again to Mississippi's shore.
They dreamed no more of boundless wealth. They felt
That all their hopes of halls and wide domains,

And rank and titles, in old Spain, were gone.

   Meanwhile disease upon De Soto came
And slowly, surely wore his life away.
With failing strength his better self came back.
She who had won and held his daring heart
Was often present in his fevered dreams.
His soul pored o'er her letters, long preserved,
And his fond Isabella's words of love
Lit up and cheered his lonely tent with light
Unseen by any mortal eye but his.
Her prayers did, doubtless, hover o'er his bed,
And gently turn his dying thoughts to God.

   I grieve, O river! that thou canst not take
Some added glory from De Soto's name.
I grieve that fortune, circumstance and time
Did ever blur and darken such a heart!
He died, a splendid wreck upon thy shore,
And deep beneath thy solemn current sleeps!
The dusky robe of midnight hung afar,
And somber clouds did move along the sky,
And here and there a weeping star looked down,
And all thy winds in sighing gust swept by,
And all thy rolling waters moaned in grief,
When thy broad bosom opened to receive
The form that bore De Soto's soul on earth!
They did not mourn because his body died;
It was because his noble soul did fall,
A withered thing before the god of gold.

IV.

MARQUETTE ON THE MISSISSIPPI.

No vestige did De Soto leave, to tell
That he had to the Mississippi marched.
By sordid hopes and passions darkly led,
He had no power or wish to lay the broad
And deep foundations of a coming State.
The stainless Spirit of eternal Truth
Would not along such leader's pathway move,
And waited yet another hundred years
And more, and Mississippi still was left
Without the sights and sounds of cultured life,
And his wide flood of waters still remained
A lonely, unappropriated waste!
But God had destined better things for thee,
O river! and thy valleys were to be
The home of labor, cities, wealth and schools.
A growing, moving Nation from the James,
And Plymouth Rock, and Carolina's sands,
Was slowly nearing Aleghany's base,
With eyes fixed on thy fair and fertile shores.
The purpose leading forth those earnest men
Demanded purer couriers in front
Than such as only sought for gems and gold;
And when that hundred years and more had
    passed,
One fully worthy of the task appeared.
Nor state, nor pomp, nor high command, was his,
Nor trappings rich with ornamental gauds.
A lowly, humble messenger he was,

In all things poor, save love and faith and grace ;
These, and the cross of Christ, his only arms.
Marquette invaded, with a fearless heart,
The wild and pathless vales and jungles deep,
Along the borders of that mighty river,
And hoped to conquer them for peace and God.

He sailed upon an Indian boat of bark,
Scarce noted and uncared-for by the world,
But by an unseen angel convoy watched,
Transcending all the hopes of earthly kings !
Southward he sailed, by rocks of monster shape,
By prairies reaching far beyond the sight,
By green and tufted islands in the stream,
And forests which had never felt the stroke
Of axe or saw. Thus southward on he sailed,
The red man seeking, that he might to him
Proclaim the gospel of the cross of Christ.

The pilgrim, landing, wandered till he found
The savage heathen in his native wilds,
And sought to win him to the fold of God.
That scene recalled is worthy all our thought :
There stood the forest stretching far away,
And there the Mississippi rolled along,
And there the red men round their wigwams sat,
And there that humble priest of God stood up,
And told to them the story of the Cross ;
And savage ears, unused to hear such sounds,
Did listen to the loving words he spake,
And savage hearts, unused to feel such truths,
Did soften under thoughts unknown before,
While from their far-off home of light and bliss

The earth's redeemed and happy throng of saints
Looked down with sympathetic eyes, and wept,
And all the sky was bright with tears of joy!
How little are the tempting things of earth,
Its greatest baubles, scepters, thrones and crowns,
To him whose spirit comprehends and feels,
In all its force, the scope of such a scene!
The service over, and his blessing left,
The pilgrim sought his bark canoe once more;
But ere he went, those forest children hung
Upon his breast the sacred Calumet,
Adorned with plumage from the brightest wings
That glanced in beauty through their vocal
  groves.

 'Twas thus from shore to shore, from tribe to
  tribe
He sailed, proclaiming Jesus every where.
'Twas thus, O Mississippi! mighty stream!
On thee he floated in his boat of bark:
But on another boat of build divine
His soul upon another river sailed,
A gleaming river, clear, serene and deep,
Of longer reach, and broader sweep than thine —
A river o'er whose waves no craft of earth
Material sail has ever yet unfurled;
And in whose depths are gems of fairer ray
Than ever gladdened any mortal sight
Or flashed in beauty on a mortal brow —
The river of eternal love and peace,
Whose waves make glad the city of our God!
So on the Mississippi passed his days
In earnest labor for his Master's cause,

Until his Master gently called him home.
No morbid clinging to the things of earth,
No fearful shrinking from the hand of fate,
No painful struggle with disease was his.
So lightly on his heart death's summons fell
None thought except himself his hour had come.
He asked one day that he might be alone —
Alone with God among the forest trees,
And there, in humble prayer and earnest hope
And all the triumph of redeeming faith,
He died; and there they made his hallowed grave;
And there by men his name was long invoked
On lake and river when the winds were high.

V.

THE PIONEERS.

By Plymouth Rock, on Carolina's sands,
And on the shores of James, was heard the tramp
Of that great Nation, building as it went,
Which in the Mississippi's valley sought
To find its final home and resting-place.
Strong men, with high and earnest hopes and
    aims —
Men who had thought and suffered, and who felt
Those pure monitions of the human soul
Which teach eternal gain as well as loss,
Were on that slow and long and weary march,
With law, religion, hope and steadfast faith;
And Truth's eternal wings of healing light

Were spread in mercy o'er their toiling way;
And Truth's eternal Spirit often wept,
Corrected and reproved, as well as praised;
For often were their thoughts and actions stained,
Oh! deeply stained, with error and with crime!
But there was strong, abiding, earnest love
Of human liberty within their souls,
And they were full of most exalted hopes,
And sought for conquest over their own hearts.
This was for them the surest way to good:
When man has learned that he is frail and weak,
And prone to evil courses still, the child
Of dark, unholy passions from his birth,
And then has learned to hate the sins that bind
The pinions of his high immortal mind,
And seeks to conquer evil thoughts and ways,
He for resulting happiness may hope.

   So, with their hearts and judgments darkened thus,
But striving still for better things, those men
Were on that long and weary march to thee,
O giant river of the western world!
But not with natural internal foes
Alone were all their hardest conflicts fought;
For old Oppression followed at their heels,
And waved its midnight banners in their rear;
And long before they finished their first march
They were compelled by force to halt and arm
And drive it back to its old haunts again.
But still, amid that conflict's wildest rage,
They turned their thoughts and hopes and hearts to thee!

Though frowning mountains crossed their onward way
And pathless forests stretched in deepest gloom,
Where cunning, warlike, savage hordes were hid,
Yet, forward still, through danger and through toil
Those earnest men moved slowly, bravely on!
They scaled the Alleghanies' craggy heights;
They cut the gloomy forests from their path;
They fiercely drove, on many fields of blood,
The savage nations of the land away;
They founded States and cities as they moved,
Until, triumphant over every foe,
Their homes were made, at last, upon the shores
Of that great river they so long had sought.
No temporary search for gold was theirs.
Their purpose was to lay an Empire's base,
And build its noble arches for all time,
And unto Freedom dedicate the work,
In His great Name Who rules the earth and sky!
And now that Empire stretches far and wide,
And covers free-born millions with its shield!

VI.

THE MISSISSIPPI AND THE STEAM ENGINE.

When that great Nation from the shores of James,
And Plymouth Rock, and Carolina's sands,

Had cleared its fields and made its homes along
The Mississippi's wide and fertile vales,
It felt the need of some compelling power
Which could his broad and rushing current make
A rolling highway for its use. The sails
That bore the fleets of nations o'er the seas
Had not the strength to breast his downward
    flow.
'Twixt Genius and unanswered wants like this,
There is creating sympathy which brings,
At last, the end desired. The great in mind
In far perspective often see such wants
Long years before the real need has come:
For Genius is the Prophet of the soul —
The instrument of inspiration used
By God for making man the architect
In building for himself a great career.
And that Eternal Wisdom which reserved
For Freedom's final resting-place the marge
And vales of that majestic river, had
Inspired some brave and clear and searching
    minds
To seek the power lying hid in steam,
And train it for the good of common men.
Those sages, oft derided by the world,
Projected many wise and thoughtful ways
Whereby that power could be evoked and used.
Although they learned not all there was to know,
Yet they did much — they labored not in vain.
Such mighty thoughts need ages for their
    growth.
The men who first conceive them make and leave
An open road, along which others walk.

They question Nature with unfearing eyes,
And, seeking all the aid that art can give,
Its darkly hidden mysteries unfold.
Thus they a broad and beaten highway make
For others' use. They are the Pioneers
Of thought, and truth is in their very dreams !
Now, what is partial failure unto them
When they can look far down the sweep of time,
And see some kindred soul their work take up,
And carry forward to a happy end ?
    Battista Porta, Edward Somerset,
Newcomen, Papin, Solomon de Caus,
With Thomas Savery, Edwards, and James Watt,
And many other men of worthy note,
Had brought the occult force of steam to light
And made, with skill, machines of high device,
Whereby its power was known in useful arts.

    But when that Nation from the shores of James,
And Plymouth Rock, and Carolina's sands,
By Mississippi had its Empire made,
There was not any Engine, breathing steam,
Or moved by any force applied by art,
Which had the might to meet and overcome
His flood of waters in their downward way !
Such Engine was a daring dream, until
The Mississippi felt that Nation's tread
Upon his shores, and called aloud on man
To organize the thought, and send it forth
A fact. The soul of Fulton heard the call,
And, by the light which other Sages left,
The matchless work was done ; and on the day
That Steamer up the Hudson's current moved,

And conquered all resisting force, there went
A thrill through all the Mississippi's waves !
That triumph was for him, for all men knew
It could not be for any meaner tide than his !

'Twas all ordained of God : He breathed upon
The glowing brain of Fulton, where were books
And cultured men to help him think and work,
And Mammon's sons to furnish means withal ;
So, in Time's fullness, forth the Engine came,
To make the Mississippi's moving breast
An inland sea, o'er which would bravely float
Great lines of Steamers with their precious
 freight !
The sympathetic touch which Genius feels,
When some great need is wanting to be met,
Did not awake the skill to do this thing
Till thronging thousands waited for it there,
Beside that noble river's bounding waves !

VII.

ANDREW JACKSON AND THE MISSISSIPPI.

The Mississippi glows with pride elate
When January's sun, each year, brings round
That memorable day on which was fought,
By Packenham and Jackson, and their men,
The first great battle that his current tinged
With blood, and waked the echoes of his vales !

About the Crescent City, New Orleans,
Still linger many stories, now grown dim,

That come in whispers through the dusky haze
Of old tradition — tales of knightly men
And lovely women — tales of bloody deeds
In fierce duello done, and legends wild
Of pirates grim, who harbored in the bays
And isles along the gulf.   Her very streets
Hold dreams of chivalry and old renown,
Floating above the noise and rush of trade—
Dreams realized and fondly treasured up
By high and gentle souls that love to think.
But that red battle fills the proudest hour
Which New Orleans has ever known.   To him,
That wise, heroic, patriotic man,
Who then our soldiers led to victory,
She renders honors when that day returns.
It is a story which will always give
Historic splendor to that city's name.

   From European conflicts legions came,
With prestige won on many hard-fought days—
Well drilled, and trained in all the points of war,
And led by sage, and brave, and skillful men.
They came to spoil her beauty and her wealth —
To light her streets with flame — to fill her homes
With wailing desolation worse than death,
And mingle with the Mississippi's voice
The wild, despairing screams of ravished maids
And matrons.*   Thus incited, on they marched,
With banners flying, and in thick array.
'Twas grand to look upon!   Their uniforms
And flashing bayonets — their well kept lines —

---

*The countersign given out by Packenham just before the battle was, "Booty and Beauty."

Their martial tread — their mien resolved and
    stern—
A scene presented fit to rouse the souls
Of all who glory in a gallant foe !
But Andrew Jackson was prepared to meet
And welcome them to death.   His untried men—
Men lately from their farms, and mills, and shops,
Men all unused to battle, and the din
Of war — blanched not nor fled when danger came;
For they were freemen fighting for their homes,
Who thought it better far to bravely die
Than live to bend before a tyrant's frown.
With kindling joy and pride, their leader saw
Defiance on each face and in each eye,
And felt, at once, that victory would be his.

  The charge is on !   The fearless Britons still
Maintain the reputation they had made
On Spanish plains and rivers far away,
And onward rush to die !   For Western guns,
In hands as fearless as their own, bring down
Their leaders and their deep embattled ranks !
But still, amid the smoke and flash and roar,
With bayonets fixed, they move upon our line,
Which with unshrinking will the issue meets
And slays them as they come !   With deadly aim
Our rifles strew the field with bleeding men
Who ne'er again shall, living, cross the sea !
Brave Packenham and Gibbs, with thousands
    more,
Are slaughtered as they make that headlong
    charge !
While, with unceasing crash, our guns still blaze,

Until, by such unequaled nerve appalled,
E'en British veterans turn and from them flee!

Our arms prevail — th' invading foe is gone —
Defeated, crushed, and flying fast away,
And New Orleans is saved from rapine, fire,
And the insulting tramp of hostile feet!
She curves in beauty with the bending shores,
Round which the Mississippi grandly sweeps,
And bears her commerce to the stormy Gulf!
There is rejoicing in her streets and halls,
For news of triumph from the battle comes;
And all her sons send forth a pealing shout
Which rises upward to the arching sky,
As he, the *Victor*, on his war-horse rides
Among them, with his deathless laurels crowned!
Great man! behold him firmly seated there,
Reining his champing steed with stately ease
And with the strength of Masterhood and Mind
Upon his rugged face! It is an hour
The Crescent City never can forget,
And which will with the Mississippi link
His name in glory that shall never die!

VIII.

THE MISSISSIPPI AND THE CIVIL WAR.

Upon our country came a time of gloom
Which all along the Mississippi scowled.
Above the States there gathered clouds of wrath;
They rolled from East to West, from West to
    East—

From North to South, from South to North, and like
A whirlwind met in fury on his shores!
The rush of battle and the storm of war
Were heard resounding with terrific force,
Throughout the length and breadth of all the land;
And why—why were our fields with blood made red
When no invading foe was on our soil?
'Twas internecine strife and civil war.
The sons of fathers who had bravely fought
In former days for freedom, side by side,
Could not agree among themselves, and hence
The rush of battle and the storm of war,
And hence the flow of blood upon our fields.

   This strife along the Mississippi raged
In part, and gave new glory to his name.
Great forts arose upon his bordering hills,
Equipped for siege and filled with armed men;
While there, opposing fleets, in iron cased,
For conflict ready, floated on his breast;
And all along his smiling banks and waves
Were heard the booming roar of mighty guns,
The crash of rifles and the battle shout;
And his deep waters crimsoned with the blood
Of fearless men who in those combats fell—
The flushing color of a rueful fame,
O'er which the chronicler must sadly weep,
Because heroic kindred madly fought
Each other when that blood was bravely shed.
Which side was right, I argue not nor say.

But this I utter with no sort of doubt:
That on no other battle-fields of earth
Was ever greater courage, greater skill
Displayed by mortal man, than in that war
By brothers waged against each other here.
Then daring deeds on either side were done,
And campaigns sagely formed and carried out,
And sieges laid with all the art of war,
And by unshrinking valor urged and met;
And battles lost and won where thousands died,
Which will along historic pages glow
In brightening splendor as the ages pass:
And names were made whose light will never dim,
But live, O Mississippi! through all time,
And glow in fadeless glory with thine own.

   There Polk, the knightly Bishop Paladin,
At high Columbus held command; McCown,
At Island Ten; at Vicksburg, Pemberton;
While Lovel led at far-off New Orleans.
All these, with many other names renowned,
Upheld the Southern banners waving there;
And first among them Bedford Forrest stood —
A soldier born — a hero every inch!
Upon the other side were soldiers true
And brave, who did on many fields sustain
The happy fortunes of the star-sprent flag.
Among them Grant was leader chief in fame.
His laurels by the Mississippi's marge
First budded—fated afterwards to bloom
And grow elsewhere to full, immortal life!
These on the shore with skill and courage fought,
While fleets upon the rolling waters met

In battle's shock, resolved to sink or win!

   In front of Memphis on a famous day
Was their last meeting. Deep and broad the
      stream—
The squadrons face to face—and soon great guns
Their volleying thunders pealed from shore to
      shore,
And miles away were through the valleys heard.
Shot after shot we sent, rebounding from
The iron-plated walls that stood opposed!
Shot after shot in fierce reply came back
That tore our weaker vessels through and
      through!
At last in full, and swift, and grand career,
They on each other rushed! Down went our fleet
Beneath the waves from which it never more
Can rise to swim and fight opposing foes!

   O mighty river! grandest of all streams!
In thy wide bosom fold with tender care
Those wrecks, once manned by high and gallant
      hearts!
Forever let them in thy waters sleep,
Unharmed by Time's destroying touch and hand!
For from them will arise the tuneful voice
Of Fame in clear, undying songs to thee!
Predestined fate was never met before
With any more determined, braver will,
Than when they sank, a sacrifice to faith
And manhood, and the glory of thy name!

   The South, outnumbered, in the contest failed.
Its tents are folded and its guns are hushed;

Its blades are sheathed ; its banners furled away ;
Its fleets, deep under water lying, sleep,
And its wild battle yell is heard no more,
But not one single blot its honor stains !
Still on the Mississsippi's flow its sons
Can look, with heads erect, and feel no shame !
It was a gallant foe that bore them down —
Of equal skill and prowess, but in all
The muniments for making wide-spread war —
In teeming armies, clothed, equipped and fed —
Exceeding far all that the South could bring.
And thus the long-protracted conflict ends,
And leaves the Mississippi flowing through
A widely reaching realm of Commonwealths
Once more united for the general good.
And I, who was upon the failing side —
Whose heart was with, and for my people beat —
Whose hope was that they might succeed, now feel
That failure was good fortune for us all !

  O great Jehovah ! God of earth and sky,
Lord of all worlds throughout the universe !
In all things infinitely strong and pure,
And wise and good ! Thou great *I AM !*
To Thee I raise my eyes, and hands and heart,
And pray that civil war may never more
Array the children of this happy land
On battle-fields in fierce opposing strife !
And that the Mississippi may move on
In peace, through all its course, beneath one flag,
Until the fated trumpet sounds the doom of Time !

IX.

THE MISSISSIPPI AT FULL FLOOD.

The Mississippi is at all times grand :
E'en in his calmest, smoothest moods his waves
Sustain, with ease, great steamers freighted deep,
Upon whose decks on breezy summer eves,
By moonlight many a tale of love is told.
But Mississippi's greatest hours are when
The floods descend in tribute to his power.
I do remember one especial time,
When I beheld him thus aroused and wild.
'Twas in the month of June some years ago,
The far-off mountain peaks, on either hand,
That stand like giant sentinels to watch
And guard the valley stretching from his shores,
Had all the winter worn their robes of snow :
But southern winds and melting showers had
  come,
With intervening days of mellow sun,
And down the mountain sides gushed sparkling
  rills
By thousands leaping to the vales below ;
Then followed, "marshaled by the thunder's
  voice,"
The summer clouds, and rain in torrents fell ;
And all the rivers of that valley rose,
And on, in fury, dashed their coursing waves !
Missouri, Arkansas and Tennessee,
The Cumberland, Ohio, Illinois,
And Red, and many other streams of lesser note,
With crested, foaming currents, poured along

Their tributary waters to their King,
Who from his mighty channel leaped in joy,
And gave them roaring welcome to his heart!
'Twas thus he gathered strength from every side
Which sent him on his wild, resistless way!
Whatever met him yielded to his force.
Uprooted forests floated on his breast;
Towns were submerged and cotton fields o'erwhelmed,
And teeming cities trembled as he passed,
And felt his waters close upon their walls!
All man's vain efforts to confine his course
Were fiercely dashed aside and spurned in scorn,
And man himself stood by in helpless awe,
And saw the ruin which he could not check!
Cyclones and clouds, emitting flaming bolts,
From all the circling heavens on him rushed
And sought in vain to force his current back!
And when the contest ended and his foes
Were overcome and driven to their lairs,
He rolled in triumph to the stormy Gulf!

X.

THE GREAT VALLEY.

Extending far and wide from either shore
In many youthful, broad and growing States,
The Mississippi's empire spreads its power.
Though often checked, disturbed, obscured and stayed,
And sometimes almost darkened into night,
It still moves onward in its great career!
The law of its development has been

Freedom to man in person and in soul.
That law, emerging from each passing storm
With fresher beauty on its healing wings,
Has ever been its watchword and its guide,
And will be in the ages yet to come.

  With what delight imagination leaps,
Rejoicing forward to the coming time
When Science, Art, and Liberty and Love,
Shall beam united on thy happy shore,
Oh! thou mightiest River of the earth!
The thoughts which in them hold these daring
      hopes
Have, sunlike, slowly risen, one by one,
In yonder weary waste of ages past,
And drifted, (driven by dogmatic creeds
And tyranny in church and state,) to thee!
Here by thy waters they have found a home;
Here by thy waters shall their strength increase;
And here in full-orbed splendor shall they rise,
Until they touch the zenith clear and blue
Of sacred Truth's empyrean sky, and thence
Shed light undimmed forever o'er the world!
Then shall thy empire, River, make return
To those old lands whence came its law of life,
And gladly send them back that law again,
Released from all retarding thongs that bound
And fettered fast to earth its youthful wings;
And then thy waves shall all their voices lift
And sing an anthem to the Triune God,
In sweeter, purer, grander melody
Than they had sung in all their years before!
Such visions of thy valley on me rush

And brighter, nobler visions still than these!
My soul is filled with high prophetic faith,
That here the New Jerusalem shall be —
That here the just and good, the pure in heart
Of every age and every creed and clime
Shall meet and wear their bright eternal crowns,
And wave their deathless palms of victory —
That here Jehovah shall unveil to man
The matchless glories of the Great White
 Throne,
And bliss immortal reign forever more!

CENTENNIAL TRIBUTE TO WASHINGTON.

July, 1876.

A thousand names around our country's birth
    In bright historic glow their fame combine;
But one there is of most exalted worth,
    Whose fragrant lustre seems almost divine:
That name remains distinct, apart, and high;
    Not comet-like, emitting baneful blights,
But, throned forever up in glory's sky,
    It shines a fixed star with its satellites.

When gloom tyrannic o'er our land was cast,
    When freemen's rights with blood and life were bought,
For us, through want, and pain, and wintry blast,
    And lying envy and defeat, he fought;
Amid the blood-red storm of battle leading,
    With one high purpose filling all his soul,
He braved each peril, hero-like, unheeding,
    Until he stood triumphant at the goal.

But his transcendent triumph was not won
    That he might wear a crown, a sceptre hold;
For liberty his noble deeds were done,
    For liberty his tide of victory rolled.
When rescued liberty in safety breathed,
    He straightway folded every standard-sheet,
His flashing brand of war forever sheathed,
    And calmly laid them at his country's feet.

A high ambition that would not endure
    The aid of any thought or action wrong,
Exalted wisdom, calm, serene and pure,
    A fortitude sedate, self-poised and strong;
The glory which from stainless honor springs,
    A valor formed to dare and overcome,
A soul proportioned for the grandest things —
    Of that unequaled man made up the sum.

With dauntless soul, and with unshrinking hand,
    He nobly wrought for us, our hero-seer,
And round him rose the pillars of the land;
    And now, in this our first centennial year,
With what full hearts, what patriotic love,
    Our minds look through the past, upon the might
With which he bravely lifted, far above
    Despotic hands, our country's Dome of Light!

His great example lives in fame sublime,
    And, like an ever-burning Pharos, gleams
In splendor by the storm-swept sea of Time,
    And on each nation's pilot throws its beams.
With gratitude earth's noblest country owns,
    How much to him its life and freedom owe;
No greater name is found among earth's thrones,
    Nor with a brighter earth's long annals glow.

MARTHA.

A COUSIN.

I.

I saw her last long years ago,
Ere Time had dimmed the sunny glow
Of youthful hope upon my brow —
Before my heart was sad as now.
　Her form was full of ease and grace;
Her dark hair glistened, and her face
Was molded in a perfect die,
And caught its beauty from her eye,
Which softly beamed with living thought,
Wherewith her mind was richly fraught.
She was imbued with that nice sense,
Which seeks and finds delight intense
In all that's pure: and those deep thrills
Of harmony whose music fills
All earth, and from its thousand hills
Floats upward to the bending skies,
And there in mellow cadence dies,
Her listening soul could plainly hear,
Although unheard by mortal ear.

II.

　She died in beauty — died ere time
Had taught her there were blight and crime —
Had taught her there were woe and strife
In all the walks and ways of life:
She died amid her own sweet dreams,
While music from the crystal streams
Of her pure thoughts sang softly clear,

And raised her far above all fear.
The forms of Beauty, Truth and Love
On gleaming wings were poised above
Her couch of death, and bore afar
Her parting soul, o'er sun and star,
High upward through the opening skies,
To endless life in Paradise.
Some grieving hearts she left in gloom
That linger still around her tomb;
Those grieving hearts were sorely riven
To give one Spirit more to Heaven —
One Spirit more of priceless worth,
Ascending from the clouds of earth.

III.

Oh! often, in that land of shade
Where dreams their mystic homes have made,
We meet, and Heaven can never be
A purer world than that to me.
No earth-born passions enter there
To taint for us its blissful air;
No earth-born clouds within it rise
To hide from us its calm blue skies:
But ever does her gentle voice
In what is good bid me rejoice,
And struggle bravely for the right,
Unchilled by fear, unawed by might:
And ever better is my heart,
And ever for a nobler part
Does my soul yearn, as far above
Her Spirit glides, in hope and love,
On graceful pinions bright and fleet,
From that dim land in which we meet.

AN OLD ARKANSAS HOMESTEAD.

Written shortly after the adoption of the Constitution of 1874.

I have designedly omitted to mention the name of the particular Homestead which suggested the following stanzas, because there were many such in South Arkansas before the late civil war, and I wish the one I have attempted to describe to stand as the representative of them all. I deem it not unmeet, if my lines deserve to live, thus to preserve for our children some idea of the rural homes of their fathers under a phase of social life which has passed away forever.

I.

The Bodcau bayou winds along,
    Through in wide pine woods forever green;
It utters but a sluggish song,
    When summer flowers its margin screen,
But rushes with a headlong roar,
When winter clouds their rain-storms pour;
Though in that soft and sunny clime
The winter stays the briefest time;
For scarce the autumn leaves have died,
When breezy spring renews their vernal pride.

II.

No mighty mountains loom up there,
    Lifting their craggy peaks on high,
Far reaching through the middle air,
In dim outline along the sky.

In softer views the landscape breaks,
Where Bodcau forms its tiny lakes;
And through its vales the wild deer roves,
And wild birds sing within its groves,
Filling the aisles with loving glee
And unpremeditated minstrelsy.

III.

Soft is the spring where Bodcau flows,
   In Arkansas far south and west,
There long the fervent summer glows,
   Bright as in "Araby the blest;"
And oh! what genial autumn skies
Around its valleys bend and rise!
While every fragrant floral bloom,
That fills the air with sweet perfume
In southern lands, is opening fair,
Through all the autumn, spring and summer,
    there.

IV.

There, by the Bodcau long ago —
   How long 'tis useless now to tell —
There, where the sweetest flowers blow,
   A rural homestead rose; a dell,
Where walnut trees and may-haws grew,
Lay to the east; while great pines threw
Their shadows on the northern side,
And on the south; and far and wide,
In many fields outstretching west,
A fresh plantation spread its fruitful breast.

V.

A rich return to labor gave
   That farm: for there the cotton plant,

Reared chiefly by the negro slave,
    Its snowy clusters waved; and Want
And Hunger, with their eyes forlorn,
Fled from its fields of bending corn:
Delicious fruitage, blood-red cherries,
The straw — most succulent of berries,
And great round peaches — tempting sight —
All ripened in its glowing summer light.

VI.

That Homestead was no castle old,
    Where knighthood dwelt and armor hung,
Nor any fierce old baron's hold,
    Whose praises courtly minstrels sung;
For such by Bodcau never rose,
And simple was the life of those
Who filled that home of long ago;
Their chief delight, to reap and sow,
And gather in their harvest stores,
And heap them proudly on their wide barn floors.

VII.

Of long pine logs, all trimmed and peeled
    And split, the house itself was made;
With riven slabs its sides were ceiled;
    With rude oak boards its roof was laid;
And chimneys, built with slush and wood,
At either end erect there stood.
The furniture was scant and rough,
But for the country quite enough,
And taste and cleanliness, in part,
Supplied the want of richness and of art.

VIII.

A double house, two stories high,
  It was, with twelve feet pass between;
Two bed-rooms formed the rear; and nigh
  The kitchen stood, well kept and clean,
Disclosing that the gentle care
Of woman's eye and hand was there;
While stag-hounds lying in the yard,
And skins of buck and bear and pard,
With shot-guns, rifles, pouches, stowed
Along the walls, the hunter's presence showed.

IX.

The ivy, climbing from the ground,
  The windows curtained o'er with green,
And wild-rose banners waved around,
  And floated out in peace, I ween.
Their only sentinels were two sweet girls,
With glowing faces, auburn curls,
Beaming blue eyes, and teeth like pearls:
These by their flowers kept faithful guard,
And ne'er was better watch and ward
Held over castle by vassal or lord!

X.

And no rude boor of villain strain
  Was he, the master of that home;
For mantling full was every vein
  With blood whose purple flow had come
From knights who fought in freedom's cause,
For England's rights and England's laws
When Cromwell, in his greatest hour,
At Naseby broke a tyrant's power;

Through knightly sires who fought again
With Green, for liberty, on Eutaw's plain.

XI.

A self-respect intuitive,
  An honest, high and fearless heart,
With all that such a heart can give,
  And such respect to man impart,
Were his; and these, without parade
Or undue self-assertion, made
His presence deeply felt by those
Who met him, whether friends or foes.
Yet on occasion he could be
Alive to frolic, fun and jollity.

XII.

His was a happy home indeed;
  A happy home where sunshine glowed,
Where truth and love in peace agreed,
  And bliss in crystal currents flowed.
The mother with her smiling face;
Her daughters, full of sweetest grace;
Two sons unmatched in field or chase;
The gray-haired father, in his pride
Easy, serene and dignified—
These were the charms of that bright fireside.

XIII.

How genial hospitality
  Did there, a constant inmate, dwell,
Unstinted, hearty, warm, and free,
  'Twould be superfluous to tell:
That was a common virtue then

To Bodcau's homes in grove and glen :
For great or small, or rich or poor,
A welcome glowed at every door ;
But *this* especial pine-log hall
In hospitality outshone them all !

XIV.

That happy home has passed away,
   That pine-log hall is desolate,
And mouldering and dank decay
   Is everywhere from door to gate ;
Rubbish is on the kitchen floor,
Half broken hangs the dairy door ;
Neglected all, the flowers are dying,
And cultureless the fields are lying,
And one wide waste is all around,
Where once a broad and fruitful farm was found !

XV.

On Belmont's bloody field one son,
   In furious battle, charging, died
Where gallant Tappan led ; and one
   By glorious Patrick Cleburne's side ;
While their old father found his rest
Upon the high embattled crest
Of Vicksburg's hills ; for there he fell,
Rent by the fragment of a shell,
Nor lived to see the bitter shame
Which there upon his bleeding country came.

XVI.

The grieving mother lingered not ;
   She sought her husband and her boys.

O God! be theirs a happy lot
   Within Thy world of peaceful joys.
But those fair sisters — where are they?
Working most bravely, day by day,
For honest bread; slaves at their call
Once came and went, and in their hall
No menial dared their words gainsay.
Though now none but themselves their words
     obey.

XVII.

Away from that sweet home of peace,
   A home that here resembled heaven —
Abode of love, contentment, ease,
   Have they gone forth, untimely driven
By war, and worse oppression still
Than that; but with unshrinking will
Their altered destiny they fill, —
Feeling, no doubt, a fond regret
For bliss they never can forget;
But though they suffer, they shall triumph yet.

XVIII.

For once again our State is free,
   And energy shall soon destroy
Those gifts of dying tyranny —
   Our poverty and debts; and joy
And hope, unfelt through many years,
Now nerve our hearts and calm our fears;
And here, where now I sit and sing
Within a ruined home, shall spring
A new prosperity — and light,

For those sweet sisters, conquer sorrow's night.*

XIX.

They are but types of thousands more,
　Far scattered through our burdened State,
Who bravely struggle to restore
　Their homes, and conquer adverse fate;
Yes! hands that from the trembling string
Were sweetest music taught to bring,
And only lightest labor knew,
Now every household duty do,
And lend to toil a soothing charm,
Which, with fresh vigor, braces manhood's arm.

XX.

Wives, Mothers, Sisters, Daughters fair!
　Ye glories of our sun-bright clime
Deserving heroes' thoughts to share,
　Worthy the proudest hour of time!
When I bethink me of the lot
Which ye have borne and murmured not,
How patient ye have been and are,
Through toil and sorrow, want and care,
My heart a loving rapture feels,
And at your feet in admiration kneels.

*The things anticipated in the eighteenth stanza, above, have been almost fully realized.

TO JULIA.

(*My Wife.*)

I.

Three times the earth around the sun
Its annual course hath quickly run,
Since we our vows of love did plight,
Upon a calm December night.
Shadows and lights, along our way,
Have shed their gloom and flashed their ray;
But joy hath greatly filled our life,
And chiefly sunny hours, dear wife,
All glad with beauty, peace and light,
Like morning breaking over night,
Have chased earth's shadows far away
And turned our darkness into day.

II.

The highest rapture earth can know —
The purest beam — the brightest glow
That ever "shone on land or sea,"
Is shining, Love, for you and me;
It brings a bliss that will not fade
When other hopes have all decayed;
We find that bliss in mutual love,
Out-sparkling all the stars above,
And sweeter far than any flower
That ever bloomed in earthly bower.

JEFFERSON DAVIS AT BUENA VISTA.

It is a furious battle day,
The fame whereof shall live for aye,
And Buena Vista's field is red
With streaming blood, and filled with dead!

While rival banners wave on high,
The meeting armies, eye to eye,
Each other's brave assaults oppose,
And in the death-strife fiercely close!

Fighting beneath their country's flag,
O'Brien, Washington and Bragg,
With deadly aim, their batt'ries play
On Santa Anna's close array;

And Sherman's guns, with flaming breath,
Breathe forth their iron hail of death;
But still thy soldiers, Mexico!
Abide the contest, blow for blow!

Although our marshaled troops are few,
Still forward moves their line of blue,
And every man is nerving well
His heart and arm, the foe to fell!

But countless odds our ranks assail!
These countless odds at length prevail,
And shattered squadrons, forced to yield,
At last are driven from the field.

While leading on his men again,
Yonder the gallant Yell is slain;
The battle's smoke their glorious pall,
There Clay, McKee and Hardin fell;

And with them fall full many braves,
Whose bones must sleep in nameless graves,
But who have freely died to-day,
The foe's advancing course to stay!

Great Rough-and-Ready! born to lead
On stricken fields where thousands bleed,
Now is the hour for all thy skill,
For all thy courage — all thy will!

On come the foemen! Sword and lance,
That through the direful struggle glance —
Musket and cannon — all combine,
To rearward bear our broken line!

The well-fought day is surely lost,
And victory crowns th' opposing host,
Unless some great, heroic soul
The tide of conflict back shall roll!

See! Davis comes! With glitt'ring brand,
Uplifted in his strong right hand,
He bravely rides, like belted knight,
Into the thickest of the fight!

Rides for the center of the strife,
Where dangers gather, death is rife,
Followed by Mississippi's sons,
With fearless tread and blazing guns!

With shout and whoop and wild hurrah,
Resounding through the din of war,
Into the battle-storm they dash,
And mingle with its roar and crash!

The adversary legions reel
When that resistless charge they feel,
And fly, defeated and undone,
And Buena Vista's field is won!

THE WARNING.

I.

The flowers of peace and love, that grow
Around the hearth-stone's cheerful glow,
Close their soft, beauteous eyes and die,
When wine's red lightning flashes by!
Ambition's dreams of high renown,
The hopes that promise glory's crown,
Man's purest thoughts, his grandest aim,
All wither in that poisoned flame!
And reason's star-bestudded rock
Itself is shivered in the shock!

II.

Oh! would you blindly sacrifice
The boon of happiness that lies,
In spite of all our grief and care,
Enwrapped in life's surroundings here?
Oh! would you sell the hopes of youth,
And immolate respect and truth,
With all that makes you free and strong,
To do the right, defy the wrong, —
Which make the mind its best thoughts well,
And laugh at failure, fate and hell?

Oh! would you barter these — the things
That find their source in virtue's springs,
And more, the birth-right of your soul—
A place in Heaven, all for the bowl?

III.

Then, if you would not, friend of mine,
Beware, beware, the sparkling wine!
The foaming glass no more fill high,
For in it death and ruin lie.
Kiss not the beaker's glowing brim;
Those gleaming beads that o'er it swim
Are but the seeds of wild despair,
Which pleasure's hand hath scattered there.
Deceit is in wine's ruby light,
Which turns at last to fearful night,
Where reeling madmen drink its waves,
With maniac mirth, o'er pauper graves.

AN ARKANSAS PREACHER'S RIDE FOR LOVE.

INTRODUCTION.

One sunny morning in last June,
When low winds sang in perfect tune,
Among the pine trees far and wide,
There met, on Bayou Mason's side,
A gay and happy throng, to walk
And fish and eat and laugh and talk,

And otherwise themselves employ,
So as to catch the greatest joy.
The larger part were young in years,
And little knew of grief or tears;
But scattered through them, here and there,
Were wrinkled brows and snow-white hair.
And one, a preacher loved by all,
Stood by a pine tree huge and tall,
And fondly watched the young and gay,
In all their guileless sport and play.
His head was white with locks of age;
Though lit his brow; his mien was sage;
And shone, with clear and happy light,
His deep gray eye, serenely bright.
"Oh! tell us," said a gentle voice,
Whose tones made every heart rejoice,
"Oh, tell us now, what vision clear
Thy spirit fills, thou dreaming seer!"
"Nothing to thee," the seer replied,
"That thou wouldst ask can be denied;
So listen — for this the vision is
Which brings to me remembered bliss:"

THE RIDE.

In mid-September, long ago,
  One cool and cloudy morn,
Disturbed and restless I arose
  Just at the break of dawn.

Out at the gate my good steed stood,
  Accoutred all complete —

My champing, gallant thoroughbred,
   Of matchless wind, and fleet.

The circuit preacher's horse, you know,
   Must be well kept and fed;
And to those preachers grace is given
   To choose the best, 'tis said.

My own, at least, was pure in blood,
   And formed for speed and power;
Of all the steeds in Chicot's vales
   He was the very flower.

A journey long before me lay,
   That must be made by night,
O'er rivers broad, through forest wide,
   To see a lady bright.

I knew that with denial cold
   She might my coming greet;
But I had well resolved to lay
   My heart's love at her feet.

I threw the reins upon his neck,
   And sprung upon my steed,
And roused him with my whip and heel,
   And rode away with speed.

The morn was dark with murky clouds
   That o'er the heavens spread;
The sky appeared in mourning clad,
   As if a star were dead.

Ere long the rain, like falling tears,

Came pouring to the ground,
And winds swept wailing through the woods,
　　With melancholy sound.

But onward through the forest's gloom,
　　Beneath the sombre sky,
My steed I pressed with whip and spur ; —
　　He sometimes seemed to fly.

My soul was dark with troubled doubts,
　　As nature's gloomy face ;
With fears that she might not receive
　　My love with loving grace.

Though all the while I knew full well,
　　The flame within my heart
Waked not a single thought or wish,
　　That could a stain impart.

And from my passion's purity
　　A glowing bliss was born,
Which, if she coldly scorned my suit,
　　Would still survive her scorn.

But oh ! I felt that I must know
　　What my fate was to be —
Must know if those blue eyes of hers
　　Would laugh or frown on me.

So onward from the Mason hills,
　　Across Bartholomew,
Saline, The Moro, Champagnolle,
　　On my good steed I flew.

THE RIDE FOR LOVE.

Right over highways, new and rough
   I rode that daring race;
Right over creeks and swamps I sped,
   With still increasing pace.

I raced against the rapid hours
   Time carried in its flight,
That I might see my lady's eyes
   Before I met the night.

That dreary day, from dawn till dusk,
   A hundred miles I rode —
When on my front the Ouachita
   At booming flood-tide flowed.

Where was the hardy ferry-man,
   And where his ferry-boat?
The one was safe and sound at home,
   The other was afloat;

Loose from the bank, 'twas drifting out
   Almost beyond my sight;
There was no way to cross, but swim
   The river in its might.

My soul rose up in all its strength,
   And would not be denied;
At touch of spur my steed plunged in,
   And swam from side to side.

No fear of current or of drift
   Of danger or of death,
Did once obtrude upon my heart,
   Or once constrain my breath.

O friends! 'twas not the natural strength
   Of courage in me then,
That made me bravely dare beyond
   The race of common men.

It was a courage springing from
   That deep pure love of mine,
Which onward forced me, heart and soul,
   To worship at its shrine.

All unexpected, unannounced,
   In garments dripping wet,
And with commingled hope and doubt,
   My lady love I met.

And without preface or delay,
   I boldly, then and there,
In passionate and burning words,
   My inner soul laid bare.

I said without parenthesis
   What I had come to say,
O'er river broad, and forest wide,
   A hundred miles that day.

And oh! with what delight I saw
   My earnest suit she felt,
With what enraptured soul I heard
   Her voice in sweet words melt.

"Your love," she said, "upon your brow
   And in your look and mien,
And beaming softly from your eyes,
   In all its worth is seen.

"And love as strong, as deep, as pure,
  As tender and as true,
Within my sympathetic heart
  Is springing up for you."

So by its own creative power,
  While glowing full and high,
My love awoke within her heart
  Her own love in reply.

O human love! if sanctified,
  The sweetest flower thou art,
That ever blooms and dies on earth,
  Within the human heart.

The bliss from that immortal love,
  Whose glory is divine
Which Faith and Hope translate to Heaven,
  Alone surpasses thine.

THE PAST.

To W. Jasper Blackburn.

That world we call the Past —
  What shadows linger there,
Of joys that bloomed but could not last,
  Of love, now all despair.

When life is growing old,
  And locks are turning gray —
When earthly hopes their wings infold,
  And from us fall away,

THE PAST.

Then to the Past we go,
   And live within its glooms
And wander down its paths of woe,
   And weep among its tombs.

We travel through its years
   Beside the dead alone,
With none to see our falling tears
   For friends who there have flown.

Those friends we ever seek,
   As through the Past we mourn ;
With their beloved shades we speak,
   Within its darksome bourn.

How sad to you and me,
   Grief-stricken and bereft,
Those spirit-meetings there would be,
   If nothing more were left.

But we can still rejoice,
   Though tears of anguish fall,
If we will only heed the voice
   Of Christ, the friend of all.

His words of ringing cheer
   The grandest hopes impart ;
In tones that fall distinct and clear,
   He tells each grieving heart.

That in the world to come,
   The pure from all the Past
Shall be united in one home —
   One common home at last.

A home of love and truth,
  Unknowing tears and strife,
A home of never-fading youth
  And everlasting life.

And so the darkest grief
  The Past within it holds,
If we but seek, through Christ, relief,
  A flower of bliss unfolds.

RESPONSE.

By W. Jasper Blackburn.

For many years I've dwelt among the tombs of
    human flowers,
Which death did wither in their bloom — their
    earliest, brightest hours;
Those blossoms one by one were plucked, until
    they all were gone,
And I was left, of all bereft, to weep, and rail,
    and moan.

That garden where these flowers grew — I linger
    in it yet;
The Past it is — but Present too, for mind cannot
    forget;
The voice, the kindly word, the call, the songs I
    used to hear,
In cadence soft and sweet, once more do greet
    my longing ear.

I touch the velvet cheeks, and kiss the silken lips again;
I praise the sparkle of an eye that never knew a pain;
I toy with hair of brown and gold, I smooth the foreheads white,
And feel that life is all a day where love doth banish night.

I rail at fate, I rail at death, implacable and base;
I feel that I could talk with God, as with man—face to face;
I feel that I could argue with the Power that took my blooms
From Home's bright Summer garden, and consigned them to the tombs.

But I have Hope of Life beyond that portal we call Death,
As strong as Faith in Christ confessed with Christian's dying breath;
It gives me strength to journey on, till with me Time shall cease,
And toil and grief are rounded with a calm of perfect peace.

"There is no death!" When those we love are carried from this world,
They pass unto another, where the soul's wings are unfurled;
The same as when they left us, there they wait our coming, when
We'll blend our loves together, and no more know grief again.

But tears fall on my pillow, when I reach and
    find them—fled ;
When I awake, and cruel truth doth tell me that
    they are dead :
I reach again, and clasp within my arms—the
    empty air !
Then o'er my soul there comes a cloud—that
    cloud of sad despair.

SONNET TO MY WIFE.

It is just twenty years ago to-day,
    Since we in wedlock joined our hopes and fears;
    How often we have mingled smiles and tears,
And griefs and joys, since then, our youthful
    May ;
And still our early love finds no decay,
    But grows more tender with the passing years :
    For us, a calmer, sweeter life appears,
The further we advance upon our way.
    How bitter it would be to quit that life,
With all its mellowing bliss, and die,
But for the light which on us breaks, as we
    Approach Time's western gates, my wife,
And through them see the sinless world on high,
Where we shall love through all Eternity.

THE GOLD AND THE DROSS.

To you, Dear, in words low and tender,
   I turn with my full soul to-night;
For only to you can I render
   My best thoughts of love and its light.

Long years have we been, love, together,
   Upon the swift river of life;
Through sunshine and dark, stormy weather
   We've passed down its waters, my wife.

Oh! surely the love that's all passion
   Is fated to coldness and gloom;
Oh! surely the love that's all passion
   In th' soul finds a desolate tomb!

We know, Dear, that true love is sweeter,
   Serener, and purer than this;
We know that the love which is sweeter
   To th' soul brings perennial bliss!

Thy form, which was lithesome and agile,
   Away in the years long ago,
Is weakened and wasted and fragile —
   Thy life-current feeble and slow.

The glow from thy face has all faded,
   The traces of age leaving now;
And never again will be braided
   The dark locks of youth on thy brow!

And low burns the love born of passion,
   Whose light like a lamp dies away!

And soon shall the love born of passion
  Go out in the night of decay!

But oh! Love, the true love and purer
  Shall never evanish in gloom!
For oh! Love, the true love and purer
  Shall fill with its glory the tomb!

Its light shall live alway in Aidem —
  The land where the soul finds its rest!
With darkness it shall not be laden,
  Away in that home of the blest!

INFANTIS HUMATIO.

Weeping we stood within the gloom
Which hangs so darkly round the tomb,
With friends who deeply felt our loss
And came to help us bear our cross,
And gave our hearts that sad relief
Which springs from sympathetic grief.
  They gently raised the coffin-lid
Which from our eyes his young face hid.
There lay the baby still in death;
No beating pulse, no balmy breath,
No winning, loving smile was there,
The mother's breaking heart to cheer.
  While standing there by corse and shroud,
With spirits anguished, broken, bowed,
Nor hoping that the hot, close night
Around our souls, excluding light,

Would ever break its clouds away,
And brighten into cheerful day—
While standing thus beside the grave,
A woman's hand, devoutly brave,
(Oh! be that hand forever blest!)
Did lay upon his little breast
A milk-white rose. No word she said,
But laid that emblem on the dead,
And o'er our hearts it sweetly shed
Celestial fragrance — hopes divine,
Which lifted them to that pure shrine,
Within the cloudless world on high,
Where flowers bloom, but never die.

We felt the babe was in that land,
And, from our hearts, we blessed the hand —
The gentle hand, and fragrant flower,
Which pointed there in that sad hour.

Oh! balmy and eternal clime,
So far above the woes of time,
Where earth's Redeemed — redeemed by grace —
Break forth in songs of endless praise,
Whose echoes through the starry spheres
Are sometimes heard by mortal ears;
May gentle hands and emblems white
Point up to thy undying light,
From every sorrow-stricken hearth
And every open grave of earth.

LUCY WOODRUFF.

A Story of the Arkansas River.

Beside the noble river Arkansas,
At Little Rock, one day long years ago,
There was a wedding ; and the brave and fair
Looked on the sacrament with happy eyes.
   The face of William Neal, the bridegroom, beamed
As if inspired by youthful life and hope ;
Interpreted by his own heart, the world
Had nothing else but peace and bliss for him.
His bride was fair as any child of earth,
Her eyes were full of loving light, her face
Like chiseled marble from the spell-touched hand
Of some old Greek, save that it glowed with life,
And had the hue of roses o'er it spread,
In delicate and almost unseen tints.
No shadow dimmed the sky which bent above
The lifted visions of their blissful souls.
Oh ! youth and love and hope and golden dreams,
How bright ye would have made this world of ours,
If ye had not been doomed to fade and die !
   Around the happy, newly wedded pair,
Came friends with warm, congratulating words ;
And mirth and wit and song their halo threw
Upon that festival of love and joy !
   Meanwhile a floating palace, newly built,
And named the River Belle, lay at the wharf.
So gently she upon the cable hung,

That none did of the mighty engine think
Which was ensconced and sleeping in her hull.
Upon her beautiful and stately form,
A score of lazy, jesting loungers looked,
And loosely talked, in that familiar way
Much used by men like them, when they do speak
Of any mind-wrought miracle of man.
They criticised her build, and spoke about
Her cost, and whether she would lose or pay,
But never dreamed what years of burning thought
Had been required to place that steamer there.
And she, unknowing of their idle words,
In queenly beauty rode at anchor, while
The bridal pageant still went bravely on.
  Just as the sun went down, the signal rang,
And from the hall the bridal train came forth,
And went aboard with all its youthful hopes.
Up from the lofty chimneys rolled the smoke,
In cloudy volumes stretching far away,
While brightly gleamed the fire within the grates
Below; and in the boiler, round and huge,
The hissing water seethed — emitting steam
Inhaled, and then respired again in jets,
By that proud steamer's mighty iron lungs.
The quick revolving wheels, beneath, obeyed
The engine's power, and the steamer moved
Upon the waters, with its precious freight.
The shores, in misty outlines, wound along,
And, from the west, the wind low music made
Upon the undulating waves. Thus went
The steamer on her way, adown the river,

While sweet young voices there, and glowing eyes,
Did send mesmeric thrills from soul to soul.
At last an old Cremona's witching voice,
Waked by a hand that knew its sweetest notes,
Made young hearts bound, and called forth happy feet
To tread the circling mazes of the dance.
  So sped the hours away, and no one dreamed
That anything but bliss was nigh — when, oh!
The startling cry rang out, "*The boat's on fire!*"
Then hushed and stilled was every sound of mirth,
And for a moment fearful silence reigned.
Then agonizing tumult broke the spell,
For there in truth the reddening horror leaped
And roared and shot its sparkling tongues around,
And flashed its eyes, and clapped its blazing hands,
And wrapped the steamer in its wings of flame.
  The pilot, cool and brave amid it all,
Breasted the steamer for the nearest land.
But what, alas! could skill and courage do?
Beneath the waters was the hoped-for shore;
The keel upon a hidden sand bed caught
Amid a forest rising from the waves!*
Hope sickened and demoniac despair
Stood, like a ghastly giant, by the flames,
And threw its pallor on each face, and men
And women shrank in terror from the sight!
Some caught the pendent branches of the trees
And climbed upon the overhanging limbs;
Some, falling, died in mortal agony;

---

*It is a fact, which may be unknown to some, that the shores of western rivers are generally low—especially towards the south; and that, in time of high water, these rivers overflow, and cover large spaces of forest lands.

Some plunged the waves, oh! never more to rise;
And some on fragments floated off to death.
Erelong the drifting clouds obscured the moon,
And chilling breezes from the northwest came,
And made the angry fire rise up and glare
Upon those pallid faces in the trees —
A fearful sight! But still more fearful yet,
A loud explosion from the steamer burst,
And roared in pealing thunder to the sky,
Commingled with despairing cries and shrieks,
While blazing fragments through the midnight
    flamed.
  Those fragments, in the water falling, died;
And then deep darkness settled o'er the scene.
There, closely clinging to the bending limbs,
With night around, those men and women sat.
There, one by one, in that cold, bitter wind,
They froze and fell into the waves below.
  At last, alone one woman there remained;
Around her female garb were closely wrapped
The garments taken from a manly form;
Only a few short hours had passed away,
Since she had stood before the bridal fane.
But where was he upon whose arm she leaned
And gave her vows? Disrobed that she might
    live,
And, falling nerveless from the tree, he died,
And left her in the freezing night alone.
  Next morning, from a steamer upward bound,
That solitary woman was descried.
The captain was informed, and launched a boat,
And had her, scarcely breathing, brought aboard.
Those river men looked rough, but in their breasts

Were true and tender hearts. Well warmed and
   wrapped,
They softly laid the sufferer down to rest.
Kindness and care and gentle stimulants
Effected much; the coursing blood returned
To her fair cheeks, and life resumed its power.
   When thus revived, she told that tale of death;
But when she came to speak of his sad fate
Who had, for her, a martyr freely died,
It was too much for her poor shattered brain;
Her eyes emitted flashing, frantic light,
And wild and incoherent words broke forth,
And she, in maniac memory, lived
Once more through all that night of dreadful woe,
While burning tears of sympathy and grief
Burst from the eyes of all who heard the tale.
Henceforth no other life she lived but that,
Until she was relieved by death. It came
In mercy soon. Before the sun had set
They bore her, cold and still and beautiful,
Back to her grieving friends within the hall
Where yesterday she stood, a happy bride.
   Oh! were it not for holy Calvary,
Oh! were it not for yonder blood-stained cross,
And yonder milk-white Banner floating out
From Heaven's blue dome o'er all the earth
   abroad,
How vain and worthless this poor life would be!
But ye, O Lucy Woodruff, William Neal,
Were Christians! and your wreck of earthly hopes
Unclosed the gates of blissful Paradise
For your ascending souls. In that pure world
Ye live united in eternal love.

THE TEMPTATION.

In yonder dreary, rugged wild,
Of barren rocks and mountains piled,
The Master slowly walked apart,
In perfect holiness of heart.

No earthly scepter filled His hand,
He owned no earthly gold or land,
He had no home, nor even bread,
Nor anywhere to lay His head.

Thus poor and lonely and distressed,
The Tempter sought to fill his breast
With longings for ambition's toys,
And dreams of earthly ease and joys:—

"If He Abaddon's power would own,
And bow before Abaddon's throne,
Then His should be the world beside,
Where He might reign in royal pride."

Though human was His birth and line,
The Master spake with strength divine:
"Get thee behind me, thing abhorred;
Thou shalt not tempt creation's Lord!"

With maddened pride, and baffled hate,
And vile malignity inflate,
The Arch-fiend fled, in fierce despair,
From Deity incarnate there.

O God! amid the sinful strife,
Which fills with woe this fleeting life,
For Jesus' sake give us the power
To conquer in temptation's hour.

GEN. McCOWN AT MURFREESBORO.

The night was still, and scarce a sound
Was heard through all the woods around;
Two mighty hosts in slumber lay,
Each dreaming of the coming fray.
The passing hours fled swiftly on,
And faintly came the early dawn,
When through our ranks from man to man
A low and eager murmur ran;
And in the keen, cold morning air,
Our battle line was marshaled there,
With banners floating free and high,
Beneath the dimly clouded sky.
"Advance!" in accents low and stern,
Makes every heart with ardor burn.
At once, amid that stirring scene,
With measured tread and daring mien,
The lines move on. No sound is heard,
Save their firm tramp upon the sward.
At first their march is calm and slow,
But each step quickens as they go,
Until, with one wild shout, they throw
Themselves, in fury, on the foe.
Without one thought of death or fear,
The Texans follow Ector here,
With their fierce battle cry; and there,
Grim Arkansas, led by McNair,
With daring charge her fame maintains;
While yonder, under gallant Raines,
The Old North State and Georgia make,
With Tennessee, the wide field shake,
And bravely cut their bloody way

Right through the foeman's thick array.
   Terrific was the conflict then !
Lines formed and broke and formed again —
The field was one wide sea of fire —
Each heart seemed filled with hate and ire —
And foes each other there defied —
And nameless heroes fiercely died —
And streams of blood from warm hearts gushed —
And on ! our charging thousands rushed
As men had never rushed before !
While, loud o'er all, the cannon's roar,
With deep, reverberating swell,
Of death and carnage told too well.
But onward, as the battle stressed,
Unflagging still, our soldiers pressed,
Until, victorious everywhere,
Their shouts of triumph filled the air,
And, ringing loudly far away,
Proclaimed them heroes of the day.
   And there, with tall and stately form,
Unmoved amid the battle storm,
Was he, whose ever watchful sight
Controlled and guided all the fight.
Oh ! surely shall the hand of fame
With deathless laurels wreathe thy name,
And, never dying, fresh renown
Shall be thy bright reward, McCown.

THE WAY.

Thought's brightest, highest, noblest theme,
Man's fairest, most delicious dream,
Is perfect moral purity —
A life from all pollution free.

And can man dare to hope for this —
For such a life, for so much bliss,
Where sinful shadows darkly fall,
A moral midnight round us all?

Ay! e'en amid this dismal night,
The soul lives on in quenchless light,
And yearns for long-lost Paradise,
And hopes at last to mount the skies.

Its plumes are soiled with earthly slime,
And trail along the shores of time;
But, gazing o'er a mystic sea,
Its eyes look on eternity,

Where those who triumph over sin
Unending life and glory win;
And all its powers at once declare
Unyielding conflict with despair.

Throughout the ages past, behold
How it has spread its wings of gold,
And fought the serpent in the dust,
For conquest o'er defiling lust.

And shall that conflict never cease,
And leave the soul in perfect peace,
Unstained by crime, sublimely pure,
And safe from sin forever more?

If man would conquer in the strife,
And rise to that unspotted life,
His soul must humbly learn to lean,
In faith, upon the great Unseen.

Through Christ, Almighty, strength is given;
By Christ, the power of sin is riven;
In Christ, the soul, supremely blest,
May find at last eternal rest.

MOLLEY STARK.

Strange things once happened unto me,
As you shall from my story see.

The wind was cool, the night was damp,
And I was sitting by my lamp,
Whose light was burning dim and low,
Emitting but a feeble glow.
The clock struck twelve. The moon was down.
The clouds swept on with flash and frown,
And at my blindless windows made
A somber, scowling, threatening shade,
While deep-voiced thunder, through the sky,
In weird and solemn tones rolled by!

With my own thoughts I sat alone;
With me to talk there was not one,
And I had thrown my books aside,
For reading I could not abide.
A glass of wine had cheered my heart;
I felt its warmth a glow impart—

Such glow as fleeting visions brings,
And vagrant, vague imaginings.
Those wild, fantastic thoughts at length,
With something like concentered strength,
Did fix themselves, as in a dream,
On Molley Stark. She was the theme
Of teeming fancies in my mind,
Of teeming fancies scarce defined;
And as I mused, it seemed to me
That an Eidolan I could see —
Eidolan of a woman pure,
Prepared to suffer, love, endure,
And fit, amid the storms of life,
To be a hero's friend and wife.

As lower burn my flickering lamp,
I seemed to hear an army's tramp,
And see another Shade appear,
And, listening, to plainly hear
A voice that rang out loud and clear,
In tones of high command, as when
A Master speaks:
     "See there, my men!"
The Shadow said with eyes alight,
"There are the red-coats, and ere night
They shall be ours, or Molley Stark
A widow!"
    Though 'twas growing dark
Within my room, still I could mark
That gallant Shade, with bearing high,
Resolved to conquer there or die!

Of Molley Stark I dreamed again —
Of what her husband said and when:

Upon that day with danger fraught,
When on the battle's front he fought,
Why was it that of her he thought?
The woman who so holds the power
On such a day, in such an hour,
To fix herself upon the heart
Of him she loves, and thus impart
Fresh courage to his soul and arm,
Must have the traits which manhood charm
To glory's way and high behest,
And life with light and hope invest.
   Now as those thoughts upon me came
Of Molley Stark's inviting fame,
Pale, shadowy forms, amid the gloom,
Were sitting all around my room;
Their dim outlines I scarce could see,
But grand those Shades appeared to me;
And that Eidolan I had seen
At first, with pure and gentle mien
Before me still was lingering there,
Above them in the glimmering air;
And in my mind I surely knew
(But how, I can not tell to you)
That this was Molley Stark again
Within the world of living men.
Before me was some rare old wine;
I saw its sparkles leap and shine;
I cut the wire, the cork flew up;
Full to the brim I filled a cup —
An ample cup with carvings nice,
A silver cup of old device —
And with the love that all should feel,
I drank to her eternal weal!

When that old wine my blood had stirred,
The battle's roar I plainly heard,
And listened to the battle shout
That over Bennington rang out;
I saw John Stark his heroes lead;
I saw the red-coats fly and bleed,
And Freedom's eagle floating there
With wings out-spread upon the air!
I filled again my empty cup —
When, lo! those Shades around stood up,
And each one poured a fragrant stream
Of nectar, with a ruby gleam,
Into a sacred, golden bowl,
And drank a health to Molley's soul!
And then those Shadows strangely grew
More palpable, and soon I knew
They were the mighty souls of those
Who triumphed o'er our British foes,
When England's proud, despotic King
Attempted on our land to bring
The darkness of his tyranny,
And bind with chains the brave and free!
Yes, those heroic souls had come
Away from their immortal home,
To drink with me to Molley Stark
Upon that stormy midnight dark!
And Molley Stark deserved it well.
For what, as you have heard me tell,
Upon a glorious day befell,
In all the catalogue of fame
We only once can find her name,
But there it glows, like some bright star,
Which fills with light its throne afar!

A HAPPY HOUR.

One day I heard a gray old man,
   (One day in early spring
While loitering among the flowers)
   In mellow tones thus sing:

The bliss of a meeting long years ago
Still brightens my heart with its beaming glow,
For starlike it shines through the night of the past,
And will while the pure and the beautiful last.

On the crest of a shaded hill I stood,
Around me spread valley, and field, and wood,
Above the horizon, round and alone,
The westering sun in its glory shone:

And a gleaming rivulet stretched away
In the golden light of the closing day,
And the wild rose trembled in leafy bowers,
Filling the air with the perfume of flowers:

And the gentlest wind, on its balmy wings
That softly and sweetly through ether sings,
With whispering cadences, music made,
And lovingly over the landscape played:

And the freshest and purest hopes of youth,
All arrayed in the hues of celestial truth,
With voices far sweeter than songs of art,
Their melodies sang in my grateful heart:

And the happiest dream the world can give,
Or the sensitive spirit of man receive,
Pervaded my soul, for there by my side
Was she whom I hoped to win for my bride.

That hour's sweet hopes have all faded away,
And she is an angel in heaven to-day;
But still its remembrance, so soft and calm,
Comes over my soul like a precious balm.

LIFE AND DEATH.

Along Life's way a shadow lies —
   A shadow falling from a form
Which floats along the Future's skies
   As darkly as a brewing storm.
It is the Gorgon men call death,
   Which on our hearts will seize some day,
And from us take our mortal breath,
   And bear our souls from earth away.
How oft we turn from all that's fair,
   With tear-bedimmed and doubting eyes,
And watch it as it floats out there —
   A Sphinx upon the Future's skies!
Does it foreshadow endless pains?
   Or shake us with alarming fright?
Or make us fear infernal chains
   In realms of groaning, hopeless night?
Yes! we can have it thus, and may,
   For Death reflects life's hues full well;
And if we live in sin's broad way
   Our dying dreams will be of Hell.
But if our lives are true and brave,
   And all aglow with beauty here,
No thought of Death or Shroud or Grave
   Can scare our souls with haggard Fear.

ARKANSAS.

The following poem was written during the pendency of the Reconstruction Government in Arkansas. In the concluding section, reference is made to political evils then existing, which were temporary, and have passed away, and, in all probability, will never be repeated. But I retain the passages, as an indication of my own sentiment, and the sentiments of a large majority of the people of the State, at the time they were written.

I.

Who does not recognize that name,
Which ever has been known to fame
Since first 'twas heard, a synonym
For daring deeds and courage grim?
Wild things, old State! are said of thee,
When thou wast in thine infancy,
Which, though they never have been sung,
Still linger on tradition's tongue;
And many hearts grow faint and sick
O'er stories told of thy tooth-pick,
And dark tales of the desperate life
Whose trust was in thy bowie-knife!
But few there are who now can tell
How bravely those old frays befell.
Then no assassin's blow was given;
The ground well chosen, weapons even;
Beneath the arching sky of heaven
Those feuds were fought, and all were free,
Who so desired, the strife to see.
All this was wrong — should not have been;
Was full of evil — full of sin;
But where on all the earth around
Can any scathless spot be found

O'er which sin's poison has not spread,
And all the springs of passion fed?
But while we sorrow o'er the crimes
Which stained and blurred those early times,
Let us rejoice that honor's law
Was then obeyed in Arkansas,
And that the fathers of our race
Despised the treacherous and base!
  Yes! Arkansas, in those old days,
Was often reckless in her ways.
Some loved a free and open fight,
At morn or noon or in the night —
A game at cards — a daring deed —
A song of love — a gallant steed —
A feast around their social boards,
There drinking like so many lords —
And a full glass of sparkling wine;
Such things to them seemed half divine!
Thus many lived a stormy life,
And gloried in carouse and strife.
But others bowed with humble hearts,
And sought the life which Christ imparts,
And listened, with attentive ear,
The preachers' songs and words to hear.
Yet, oh! no cringing hinds were they,
But men whose fearless hands would slay
The tyrant who should do them wrong,
However brave, or great, or strong!
But best of all they loved the chase —
The wild, exciting, daring race,
In full speed, after buck or bear,
Forth routed from the hidden lair.
To them 'twas sweet to hear at morn

The music of the hunter's horn —
To hear the baying of the pack,
Restless to find the victim's track —
To see the steeds with flowing mane,
Prepared to sweep o'er hill and plain,
And bear their riders to the front,
Through all the changes of the hunt !
But grander still to see the break —
To feel the hills and valleys shake —
And hear the hounds' exulting cry,
Echoing to the bending sky,
And, with exulting voice, ring out,
Each huntsman pealing whoop and shout !
Oh, gallant hearts ! I loved them well,
And on their memory fondly dwell !
As quick in kindness as in fray,
They lived in hospitable way.
When want and sorrow made demand
They ever had an open hand ;
And, ever generous as brave,
A wrong atoned for they forgave.
And in their love of womanhood
Their souls were ever true and good;
No bestial lust, no gross desire ;
It burned, a purifying fire,
Along their wild and rugged ways,
Serene and pure as diamond rays !
Such men are ever made by Fate
The fathers of a mighty State.

   Of reckless mood, unknowing fear,
In honor high, in love sincere,
O Arkansas ! thy first sons had
A checkered life of good and bad ;

And while their sins we seek to shun,
Be honor still our shield and sun;
Still in our hearts let courage glow,
And love like theirs our souls o'erflow!
    Oh! let the virtues of our sires
        Be still our guiding light —
    Be still the lofty signal fires
        Illumining the height
    Where stands the goal of our desires —
        The never dying right!

II.

  Such lives of honor and of error,
Such scenes of love, such deeds of terror,
Are not the only things whereby
Our noble State claims prestige high.
Though often, in unchristian mood,
She washed out fancied wrongs with blood,
Yet not in private war alone
Her fierce and steady valor shone.
For, still along your slopes, Oak Hills,
The story of her daring thrills!
There Churchill's horsemen, charging, go
With dauntless courage on the foe!
There Woodruff's battery, pealing loud,
Makes lightning on the battle-cloud;
And all her sons there on the field,
With high-wrought courage firmly steeled,
Do their full duty in the fray
And drive their foeman far away!
From Shiloh, Corinth, and Elkhorn,
Afar her battle cry is borne
On glory's winds, to high renown;

And yonder, under old McCown,
On Murfreesboro's well tried plain,
Right at the foe, o'er heaps of slain,
Behold her soldiers charging there,
Led on by Reynolds and McNair;
At Chickamauga, stream of death!
She bravely yielded blood and breath,
And, Ringold! on thy rocky height
She saved our army in its flight;
O'er twenty fields of victory,
Thy sword she followed, Robert Lee!
At Franklin, by the Harpeth's shore,
Amid the conflict's wildest roar —
On that red front of battle leading,
Where men, on every side, are bleeding,
See how heroic Cleburne dies,
As his brave foe before him flies;
But oh! his deeds shall ever live
In all the luster fame can give.

  On other days Arkansans led,
In other battles freely bled —
Defending with a dying hand
Their homes, their rights, their native land.

  Old State! thus have thy heroes died
And thus their blood has fructified
Great fields of death, whose names shall ring
In song, with thine, while bards can sing.

    That fame is ours in sacred trust
      And we must keep it pure;
    No action born of servile lust,
      Can such a trust secure;
    No coward, licking of the dust,
      Can such a trust endure.

III.

But not alone on fields of glory
Old Arkansas has won her story.
When dreaming bards their great harps strike,
Few wake a nobler strain than Pike;
And every line by Noland writ,
Flew forth, a well aimed shaft of wit.
In yonder lofty Halls of State,
Where Titans held their high debate,
When Genius opened wide their doors,
And flashed its splendor from their floors —
In those old days, long passed away,
Superbly by the side of Clay,
Loomed Ahley's form, and in Sevier
The proudest statesman found a peer,
And stainless Johnson's voice rang clear
For right and justice, without fear.*

So rose our State, in that great hour,
When Faith and Honor led to power.
Her eagles, then, those high halls sought —
Thence soaring to the sky of thought.
But, Arkansas, oh! weep not thou,
Though vultures fill their places now,
Thy sons those vultures never were;
Thy people did not send them there;
And not by any act of thine

---

*Our State has produced few, if any, men superior to Robert W. Johnson. Both in the House of Representatives and the Senate of the United States, he occupied a high position, and also in the Confederate Senate. He was finely educated, and had thought much. Though not so brilliant as some of our statesmen in speech, his logic was clear and strong. He was as brave as "Caius Julius, the first bald Cæsar," and as irreproachable as Bayard. I have tried to express myself about him in verse and have failed, as the couplet above will show; and must therefore be content with this note

They there in putrid splendor shine!
It is a lying mockery,
Which all men most distinctly see,
That say thy name they represent,
In any place, by thy consent;
Chained to the rock thou art to-day,
And on thy life those vultures prey;
Their infamy, so widely known,
Is none of thine, but all their own.
In thy proud history, noble State,
Thy glory lives securely great,
And glows, in quenchless light complete,
Above those vultures of the street.
  Oh! guard that heritage of fame
   From out the storied past,
  Which, Arkansas! surrounds thy name,
   And will the world out-last;
And may thy children never shame
  A fame so grandly cast.

A SERENADE.

When the stars are gladly shining,
 In cloudless brightness o'er the sky,
All that's beautiful combining,
 To meet the upward gazing eye;

When the moon's pale light is glancing
 Upon the silver flowing stream,
And the tiny waves go dancing
 Beneath the beauty of its gleam;

When the breeze has hushed its singing,
   And all the forest leaves are still,
And we only hear the ringing
   Of leaping waters in the rill;

Then, oh, then, sweet girl, beside thee,
   I'd sit beneath the vining rose,
Or among the flowers guide thee,
   And all my tender thoughts disclose.

LOVE AND BEAUTY.

Everywhere there's beauty,
   Around us and on high,
For God has left His touch divine.
   Upon the earth and sky.

With feeling most delicious,
   Our souls drink beauty in,
When love is true, unselfish, pure,
   And undefiled by sin.

Alone through love can beauty
   Its sweetest bliss impart,
And wake the purest joys that sleep
   Within the human heart.

WITHOUT GOD IN THE WORLD.

O human hearts, however strong,
However brave against the wrong,
You must not in your strength proclaim
That God exists alone in name.

For know ye not that human might,
When unassisted by the Light,
Must ever be, has ever been,
Unequal to the war with sin?

In all the universe around,
For you no resting-place is found,
If you, in suborned pride, deny
The true and living God on high.

A HYMN OF LOVE.

Within our hearts let's keep the charm
   Of deep, abiding love
For all that's beautiful on earth,
   And all that's pure above.

While hate can rob the fairest things
   Of all their power to cheer,
Love glorifies the darkest hour,
   And casts out every fear.

It clears away the clouds of wrath,
   Whence springs our bitter strife,
And fills us with heroic strength,
   To bear the ills of life.

It is a purifying power —
   A light from God on high,
And falls, in peace, upon our hearts,
   Like sunshine from the sky.

Oh! may it round our hearth-stones glow,
   And linger in each voice,
And exorcise all baneful thoughts,
   And make our souls rejoice.

JOHN G. WHITTIER.

Entranced is every listening ear
   By Whittier's noble song,
Where glowing numbers, soft and clear,
   Their melody prolong;
But this does not the most impart
   Its genial influence to my heart.

It is the love outflowing there,
   In waves of living thought,
For all that's true and purely fair,
   For all by Jesus taught,
Which holds me, spell-bound, o'er the page
   Of that New England Quaker Sage.

LINES TO MISS TOM CLARK.

(Now Mrs. Milburn.)

I.

Oh ! that my pen could now indite
Some talismanic word of light
Upon this page, with power to charm
From human hearts the touch of harm —
Then all thy coming life should be
From every pang of sorrow free.

II.

Such words, alas ! no pen of man
Hath ever writ, or ever can.
Though blest with hope, and friends, and home,
Our days of brooding gloom will come;
Each heart of earth must ache with cares;
We all must shed predestined tears.

III.

But from the harp by David strung
Celestial strains of music rung,
Inspired by Heaven's own Paraclete,
In tones that e'en made sorrow sweet.
Oh ! may your soul that music fill,
And mingle bliss with every ill !

FAITH.

If God's believing children had to wait
For their reward from human tongues and hands,
Then would their lives be sad and dark indeed.

But oh! with what unspeakable delight
Do those whose earnest labors look to good
Imbibe the soft, delicious sense of bliss,
Which, independent of the world around,
Flows sweetly from abiding faith in God!
   Man may deny it blindly if he will,
And live as though it were a holy lie;
But still it is an everlasting truth,
Instinct with wisdom, infinite, divine,
That meek submission to the will of God,
In faith, brings better, brighter things to men
Than learning, pleasure, wealth, or power can.
It is a grand and everlasting fact,
Which evil never can eradicate,
That any isolated child of earth,
The lowest, meanest, weakest of them all,
Can, through the grace and aid of God, assert
His conquest over every earthly ill,
And rise triumphant master over fate,
And conquer all opposing elements
Which lie between himself and present bliss.
It is a grand and everlasting fact,
Which pride, and lust, and human vanity
Can neither darken, weaken nor destroy,
That humble, loving, trusting purity
Does bring its own reward, e'en now and here.
   And these are facts which do not rest alone
On *other* arguments for their support,
But *prove themselves* to every human heart
Which finds the humble daring thus to trust.
   Let him who doubts these facts the test apply,
And find that all the truths which shape our fate,

And radiate the deathless soul of man,
Do not, within the darkened, narrow scope
Of poor, uncertain human logic lie.

THE OUACHITA.

All rivers have a language of their own,
Whose meaning to the listening mind is known;
They have a music which can soothe the soul,
Or stir it with exhilarating roll.
That language and that music I have heard,
And they have thus my spirit soothed and stirred,
While looking on the Ouachita. Its voice,
In lonely hours, has made my heart rejoice
When not another human face was near
To break the spell, or in its happiness to share.

II.

In youth I roamed along its winding shores,
Or sped my rocking boat, with dripping oars,
Upon its current gleaming clear and fair,
In the cool glow of spring's delicious air.
I held the rod and made the cast, elate;
And then some hungry trout would seize the bait,
And bear away the line with whizzing glance,
And make it through the yielding water dance!
No tongue can tell — no pen can ever write
The deep and thrilling ecstasy of that delight!

III.

Oft by the Ouachita for social joys
We gathered — maids and matrons, men and
    boys —
And there in laughter, song, and converse, passed
The flying hours, too full of bliss to last !
There friendships grew which only death has
    ended;
There budding loves first bloomed, which lives
    have blended
For good or ill. Oh ! fleeting summer days
Of happiness, your memory with me stays,
And with that memory is the gentle flow
Of Ouachita in all its laughing, cheering glow !

IV.

The Ouachita ! how musical the word,
And with what rapture by my soul 'tis heard,
As on my listening ear it softly falls,
When recollection that sweet name recalls !
Nor time, nor absence, nor approaching age,
Can for its graceful course my love assuage !
My heart will always dwell beside that stream,
And of its waves my soul will ever dream !
Oh ! may thy living waters sing forever
Their holy songs of peace and joy, beloved
    River !

GEN. W. T. SHERMAN.

All cold and still a hero lies in death!
His arms are folded and his eye-lids closed!
That stately form, which mighty armies led,
Will never walk again the path of life!
That voice, which erst o'er battle-fields rang
    out,
Will never more be heard by mortal ear!
  Death is as old as Sin, but always new;
For he permits not living men to be
Familiar with him; though, each passing hour,
They see the ravages he makes. His shapes
Are changing constantly, and fascinate
Our minds with myst'ry, and most solemn
    thoughts.
But never is his Specter seen so far,
And never does his Shadow fall upon
So many hearts as when a great man dies
Amid a Nation's tears and wailing grief—
Such tearful griefs as now his country feels
For Sherman, lying dead upon his bier!
And I, an humble soldier of the South—
One who beheld his legions marshaled forth
For battle—one who watched their toiling way
From wrecked Atlanta to the far-off sea,
And wished for power to crush them as they
    marched—
Do sorrow most sincerely for the man,
While thinking on the shroud that wraps his
    clay!
  When he was making war upon the South,

GEN. W. T SHERMAN.

We would have gladly slain him if we could,
Upon some fair and open battle-field;
For he was then our foeman, and we fought
For rights which we believed to be our own.
But let it not be thought, for 'tis not true,
That we, the people of this sunny land,
Can see no greatness in the deeds of those
Who met us in the bloody argument
Of war.   No soldier on the other side,
Who did his duty like a man, but has
Received the just respect of all our hearts;
And those who thought and planned with skill,
    and stood
The brunt of danger with determined minds,
Our admiration; and, no doubt, the soul
Of Sherman feels a deep regard for those
Who often fought him when he failed to win.
His final triumph over men like them
Gives added luster to the bays he wears!
   From those who know the history of his life,
It is no cringing flattery to say
That he was great, and that his name will live
Among the foremost soldiers of all time,
And that his fame will aid in making up
The sum of glory due to all the States,
Again united in the bonds of peace.
So let the tolling knell that sounds his death
Be rung where'er the eagled banner flies,
And all the people sadly join as one
In doing honor to his warlike Shade!

GENERAL JOSEPH E. JOHNSTON.

Resplendent names, whose light is clear, and
    free
From taint, I love to write upon my page.
The contemplation of them there awakes
Delight within my heart, and makes me feel
That Human Nature has the elements
Of greatness in it, and recalls the fact
That man is not all sordid, low and mean;
That he can curb his grosser appetites,
And, rising o'er his low, unholy thoughts,
Can purify his mental, moral wings,
In an ethereal sea of cloudless light.

  When any one, who such a life has lived,
Departs, sorrow pervades the earth with gloom,
As though the sun himself in full eclipse
Had faded out — as though the world had lost
A treasured blessing which it could not spare.
For such a loss we mourn. No nobler man
Has from among us gone than Johnston was.
We loved him well for what he was and did;
We loved him for his kind and gentle ways;
We loved him for his great, unselfish soul;
We loved him for his gallant heart, which oft
Impelled him on the field to coolly go
Where Danger threw its scathing bolts around,
And Death was mowing with its bloody scythe!
Ten glorious scars his Coat of Arms made up,
And each attests his courage well!

                                      He was
A soldier born and bred. In youth he fought

Among the Everglades of Florida,
And bled in battle with the Seminoles.
He followed Winfield Scott from Vera Cruz
To Mexico, there winning much renown
On every hand. Upon the craggy heights
Of Cerro Gordo, at Chepultepec,
Contreras, Churubusco and del Rey,
And in the struggles for the City's gates
He was among the foremost always found,
A leader bravely doing his devoir —
Thinking, perhaps, of other days long past,
When Cortez and his steel-clad Spaniards fought
The Montezuma there. Inspired alone
By sordid love of gold and lust for power,
They came with ruin, slavery and the torch;
We brought protection to our beaten foe;
And thus the laurels won by him whose name
I celebrate, were left untarnished by
A stain.

But he was destined yet to win
A higher fame, to act the hero on
A broader field, and in a mightier strife
To play a leading part before the world.
Our wide-spread internecine war, which shook
The continent from sea to sea, came on
And called him forth to lead again in arms.

Along the Shenandoah his forces lay,
Confronting Patterson, when Beauregard
Was near Manassas standing face to face
With that great army which McDowell led
Toward Richmond.

Watch the skill with which he foils
Intrepid Patterson, and finds his way
To where the first great conflict is to be!
Watch him, as with a leader's searching glance
He scans the field, and seizes on each point
Of vantage! Watch him, as he sends his troops
Where they are needed most, and where the foe
Is pressing on! Such men as Ewell, Bee
And Longstreet; Stonewall Jackson, Pendleton
And Early; Hampton, Evans, Bonham, Smith,
And others of the same determined mold,
He hurls in fury on his foeman's lines
With all the prescience of a General born!
Although his foes are brave and handled well,
Although they fight with true, heroic will,
They cannot stand before these timely blows
So finely given under his own eye!
At last they wildly break and flee away,
And he remains grand victor of the field!

McClellan's army moved from Fort Monroe,
Marching a hundred thousand strong and more;
And "On to Richmond!" was their battle cry.
With fifty thousand Johnston him opposed,
And held him back with ease until he reached
The Chickahominy, a name now made
Most famous; for 'twas there that Johnston turned,
And there delivered battle with such skill
And energy as made the world confess
Him equal to the greatest things in war.
That host which sought for Richmond's overthrow,
He beat and backward forced in blood and rout,

And all the wild confusion of defeat!
But while he cheered his men upon the front
And urged them forward in the hot pursuit,
Yes! just as victory crowned his arms, he fell —
He fell all bleeding from a ghastly wound!

Long months he lay disabled by that wound.
Restored to health, we find him further South;
And everywhere he does what can be done
By genius with the means at his command.

Bragg's army, shattered by the mighty arm
Of Grant at Chattanooga, helpless lay
At Dalton, all disorganized, half armed,
Half fed, half clothed, and stricken by disease,
And overshadowed by a brave despair!
But when great Johnston came and took command,
Their hearts once more beat high with hope.
They felt
That they were now to follow one who knew
The way to lead. New light flashed from the eyes
Of all those ragged heroes; and again
Was heard the battle yell which they had sent
Far ringing over many a field of death!

Sherman advanced, and all the world looked on,
For giants were about to meet; not those
Poor giants who depend alone on strength
Of body, brawn and sinew; but the great
In soul, in mind, and in the art of war —
Giants in thought and execution; for
Johnston and Sherman were such men; such men

They had for their lieutenants ; and each led
As brave a host as ever trod a field.
But still that war upon unequal terms
Was made ; for Sherman's thronging army corps
Were well appointed, and outnumbered far
The forces Johnston had to meet him with.
Had it been otherwise, the issue would
Have never for a moment been in doubt.

   The strife began. The game of war was played
By skillful hands and fearless hearts. For months
The blaze of rifles and the flash of swords
And the cold gleam of deadly bayonets
Were seen, and the loud roar of mighty guns
Was heard. Sherman, avoiding battle straight,
Sought by his skillful movements on our flanks
To wear us out and capture all our men.
But he was met and foiled on every side ;
For Johnston watched him with a wary eye,
And with the glance of genius saw his plans,
And spoiled them ere they could be carried out.
But oh ! how well and fiercely Johnston struck
When his great foeman left a point exposed,
Or made direct attack upon his lines,
Let Kennesaw, Resaca, New Hope, tell !

   And thus from month to month the strife went on
From Dalton to Atlanta. Sherman, with
His better arms and stronger force of men,
Pressed Johnston slowly backward day by day ;
But every inch of ground was bought with blood !
Johnston lost nothing in that long retreat,
Except his killed or shattered heroes, whom
We weep, and will as long as gallant men

Who for their country fall may claim a tear!
Naught else he lost; no tent, no sword, no gun,
Nor any captured banner won in fight,
Not e'en a wagon wheel, was left with which
To grace the march of Sherman's serried ranks!

But this career was sadly doomed to end;
For he was taken from the men who thought
That it was right to die at his command —
Men who believed in him and loved him well.

But when the tragic end was near, once more
They found him at their head; and even then
He made the parting days of that great war
Bright with the light of noble deeds in arms!
He closed, at Bentonville, those scenes of blood,
Amid the storm and shout of victory!
These are the facts of history that shine
In scintillating glory round his name
Before the watching eyes of all the world!

And yet he loved not war for its own sake.
No selfish, low ambition urged him on;
'Twas always at his country's call he fought,
And when to further fight was hopeless he
Insisted that the flow of blood should cease.
Considerate of others, kind in heart,
Not even gentle Philip Sidney's self
Was more sincerely courteous unto all.
His life was free from mean, unholy aims
And thoughts, as Chevalier de Bayard's was:
And when the eye of History turns upon
The sky of fame, in ages yet to come,
No brighter constellation there will flame
Than that in which the name of Johnston glows!

THE HILLS OF HICKMAN.

I.

To Hickman County, Tennessee
(Whose hills are ever dear to me,
Home, where my childhood passed away),
My thoughts in mem'ry often stray,
And linger long, with tender look,
By every garden, field and brook.

II.

O hills of Hickman! from my heart
Its love for you can never part!
Once more beneath your chestnut trees
(Whose nuts, out-shaken by the breeze,
Come falling swiftly to the ground,
With pattering and gentle sound)
I stand in thought, and dream my name
Shall surely fill the trump of fame,
As I did dream in my young years,
Without a sense of doubts or fears.

III.

On Hickman's hills, by fancy's light,
I climb again each craggy height,
And wander down their slopes and dales,
And through the meadows in the vales,
With friends whose hearts have long been cold
In death, and turned to senseless mold;
But whose pure souls shall live forever,
Along the shores of some bright river,
With waves that darken never! never!

IV.

I think of her, with auburn hair,
And deep blue eyes, and face so fair,
And lips so sweet, whom I loved there
Among those hills, in that glad time,
When youth was in its glowing prime —
Though many years have passed away,
Since first I felt that passion's sway.

V

The hills of Hickman! yes, they rise,
In blue outline along the skies,
Before my yearning, dreaming eyes,
Just as I saw them long ago,
When life with hope was all aglow;
I see again the vales between,
Rejoicing in the sunny sheen;
My listening ear, though far away
From that sweet spot of childhood's day,
In fancy hears the leaping rills
That sparkle down those well loved hills,
While tongues that have been silent long
Their echoes wake again with song;
And in my constant soul shall stay
That vision of those hills alway.

VI.

Now, in the sunset of my life,
While looking back through years of strife,
Where good and evil meet and blend —
From my full heart I gladly send
My farewell greetings unto thee,
O Hickman County, Tennessee.

THE STARS.

The Stars ! the Stars ! With holy light
They fill the sapphire arch of night !
  With love and joy profound, we sigh,
  When looking on them in the sky !
Upon their far, unmeasured height,
Forever calm, forever bright,
They glow serenely on our sight,
  In beauty which will never die —
        The Stars ! the Stars !

While passing ages, in their flight,
Of constant earthly changes write,
  They are the same to every eye,
  And still remain unchanged on high,
In deathless glory all bedight —
        The Stars ! the Stars !

COMPENSATION. *

"The mind is its own place, and in itself
Can make a Heaven of hell, a hell of Heaven."
        — *Milton.*

  He "through long days of labor,
    And nights devoid of ease,
  Still heard in his soul the music
    Of wonderful melodies."
        — *Longfellow.*

We hear men say, with pessimistic sigh,
That oft the Great in soul, the True and High

---

* Half the subject is suppressed, because I do not wish to enter upon its relations to the "earthly, sensual, devilish" soul and mind.

Without their proper recognition die,
And thus forever lose the joy that flows
From praise deserved, and from the light that
  glows
"On glory's plume;" and it is also said
That they do sometimes know the want of bread.
All this is true. But there is recompense,
Proceeding from a more delicious sense
Than any wakened by the touch of gold,
Or any which man's praises can unfold,
To him who worships in the shrine of thought
With pure and lofty purpose richly fraught.
For Genius, sanctified to some great end,
Does not for peace and happiness depend
Upon the gold and praise of earth; and those,
Who fondly grieve about its cares and woes,
Seem wholly to forget that daring Mind
A sure and constant good can always find
In that great struggle it is formed to wage
Amid contending thoughts from age to age.
While thus employed in close and deep debate,
It is prepared to bravely work and wait,
With something of the patience Gilder saw
In the eternal Mind, a holy law,
What time he looked upon a land that lay
In silence underneath the sun's broad ray,
Through which two rivers poured with currents
  free —
Their long way winding to the far-off sea.

Of course if wealth and fame do come to bless,
At once, with something of their happiness,
The lives of those who think with mighty brain,

And strive the Truth to find in glorious pain,
'T is well. But they do seek for better things —
Seek for the splendid blessedness that springs
From some unfolding thought, for its own sake,
And for the cheering hope that it may make
Light for the world! To them how grand it is,
How charged with full, ecstatic, sinless bliss,
To feel such thought emerging from the mind,
Which for itself a star-like path may find,
And there forever orb its light on high,
And move in splendor through the mental sky,
Around the glowing center of all Truth,
The Mind of God, in never dying youth!
Such joy will always more than compensate
For sorrow, want, neglect, and even hate.

 But not to those alone whose thoughts can spring
Aloft on fearless, strong and gleaming wing,
Shall come that soothing compensating joy
Which all earth's darkness never can destroy;
For Worth, however lowly be its state,
Will share, to its full compass, with the Great
In all the rapture Nature's Law can give
To those who fearlessly and rightly live.
But whosoever such a boon would win
Must fully arm his soul for war with sin;
Must gather wisdom from the Seers of old,
Whose mighty words the way of life unfold.
That all are prone to sin we fully know,
Whether by falling, or created so.
It is through painful, constant conflict here,
Through suffering, anguish, tears and mortal care,

That we must find our final happiness;
'Tis thus Eternal Wisdom seeks to bless.
He who against himself has strongly fought
To do the thing which he believes he ought
To do for good, shall feel a blessed ease,
And in his soul the sweetest harmonies
Shall breathe, like music over star-lit seas,
When all the winds are low, and through the sky
Angelic numbers seem to swell and die.
This bliss no earthly fortune can deny
To him; through it he rises, free and strong,
In happy triumph over every wrong.
Men whose mean thoughts are "centered all in self,"
Whose labors only seek to gather pelf,
Who live for low and fleshly appetite,
And who in sensual joys alone delight —
Men who are careless of the lot and life
Of other men, if they, amid the strife,
Can have success and grow, may laugh at this —
Deride and scorn the hope of such a bliss.
But oh! ye hardened, darkened, selfish men,
Dream not that you the best of life can ken;
For everywhere, from all the ages past,
And now on earth, there is an army vast
Through whose pure hearts in rhythmic measures flow
Soul songs of joy, of which you nothing know —
Which you have never heard, and never can,
Until you learn the full capacity of man
For such high things. You have not seen the height
To which the pure in heart can rise, the light

That gleams in glory there, nor found the deep
Of your own souls, where pearls of beauty sleep.
In living *right*, in doing what we *should*,
Say what you will, there *is* a constant good,
"What'er befall" us — whether burdened by
Distress or meeting, in the eyes of men, success.

 But there is grander compensation yet
For every one whose heart is bravely set
To make earth better, elevate his race,
And bring it to a higher, purer place.
Though he may only meet with cold disdain,
And, all forgotten, pass away in pain,
His soul can never die, and when made free,
By death, from its gross, earthly frame, will see,
And hear, and feel, and know, with deeper sense,
With comprehension clearer, more intense,
All things that happen on this earthly sphere,
Than while it lingered in the body here.
And, therefore, if the light of glory's flame
Shall gleam in lambent beauty round his name,
And make it brilliant as a new-born star,
Attracting admiration from afar
Long after death, although in life denied,
'Twill be more sweet to him than if he had not
  died.

 But let the worst befall, let earth forget,
Let life and mem'ry pass without regret,
And earth's oblivion darkly fold and keep
His name within a long unbroken sleep,
Still all th' Immortals shall his merit own,
And there among them he shall have his throne,
And shall, his sentient, happy being through,

Feel pure, eternal joy, the token due
And fine result of LAW, received by Worth
For pure and noble thoughts and deeds on
    earth. *

HEAVEN.

What are earth's honors and its fame,
And what "the magic of a name,"
And what the miser's shining hoard,
To him who bows before the Lord —
To him whose soul has daily striven
To educate itself for Heaven?
Immortal joy is in that work !
And all the melting heart is stirred,
When Faith can pierce the earth-born cloud
Which veils its beauty like a shroud,
And fill the soul with visions fair
Of all that seers have promised, there !

To wander through its vales of rest
In happy converse with the blest ;
To see its peaks of glory rise
Beneath its calm, ethereal skies ;
To live beside the GREAT WHITE THRONE,
Where sits the TRIUNE GOD alone,

---

* I do not mean to support Pelagianism in the foregoing poem, for I believe that the grace, mercy and Holy Spirit of God are required, as assisting forces, to enable man to work out his moral and spiritual regeneration. But I further believe that these forces are always and necessarily present and active ; and that, therefore, man can always, if he will, as certainly accomplish moral and spiritual rectitude as if he had the innate power to do so.

And bathe the soul in Love's pure river,
Which sparkles from its base forever;
To feel the bliss of sinless life,
The absence of satanic strife,
Of night and crime and tears;
To hear the music of the spheres
In symphony arise and swell
O'er fields of fadeless Asphodel —
'Tis blissful visions such as these
Which each rapt soul while musing sees,
That raise our hopes above earth's skies,
And fill our human hearts and eyes
With sweeter joys than ever came
From worldly pleasure, wealth or fame!

   O, beautiful and sinless Clime —
Home where no poisoning serpent's slime
Can ever come, with its dark stain,
To fill the soul with burning pain!
What rapture glows upon my brow,
Whene'er I feel, as I feel now,
That I shall all Thy glories see,
And live forever, part of Thee!

TO JULIA G. SMOOTE.

I.

The first and dearest name this book contains
Among its rhymes, still in my heart remains;
And, my beloved Julia, it shall stand
The last indited for it by my hand;

And may it be the last upon my lips
When mortal life is passing under death's
    eclipse.—
If thou shalt find the strength to still live on,
A benison to earth, when I am gone,
Then often read these lines by night and day,
And do not think my Spirit far away;
   For I will linger near thee still,
And turn to pearls of bliss thy falling tears,
   (If it shall be God's holy will)
And calm thy doubts and fears.

II.

I wish to speak what I do know of thee,
To tell the world what thou hast been to me.—
About love's charms there have been said and
    sung
Full many things by human pen and tongue.
Its praises have been chanted through all time,
And every land of earth, in prose and rhyme;
But long and chiefly have its votaries dwelt
Upon its lower, sensual phase, and only felt,
Or seemed to feel, no deeper, purer bliss
Within its bright dominion glows, than this.
   But we accept not what they teach,
For we do know it has a nobler height —
   A fuller meaning — wider reach —
A fairer, sweeter light.

III.

To see the health, and strength, and easy grace,
We often find in human forms — a face

All bright, symmetrically shaped, and sweet,
Where all our thoughts and dreams of beauty
    meet ;
To look into the clear and shining deep
Of some soft eye, where passions tremble as
    they sleep,
I do concede to be a happy boon.
Yet these things fade and pass away so soon
(Leaving decrepitude and age behind),
That love, in them, no permanence can find.
    But from the Spirit's graces springs
A love triumphant over every blight,
    And lighting, with its halcyon wings,
The gloom of sorrow's night.

IV.

It is this love, which in the soul finds life,
That thou hast always had for me, my wife.
Whenever happiness has been my part,
That happiness has lighted up thy heart.
In hours of darkness, sickness and distress,
How gently thou hast soothed me with thy soft
    caress ;
When petulant from pain, thy winning voice
Like David's harp, has made my soul rejoice,
And from me all tormenting fiends beguiled,
And left me like a toy-delighted child.
    Such hast thou been to me, and art ;
But human language never can express
    All thy deep tenderness of heart,
Or all thy power to bless.

V.

But that which gives the most delight to me,
Is on thy face and in thine eye to see
The light of peace, and love, and joy aglow. —
To feel that thou art happy and to know
That thy pure soul is beautifully calm,
Brings to my own most soothing and delicious balm.
Oh ! I have often seen thee thus, and felt
As though my heart in bliss serene would melt !
All joyous things which I have found in life,
And all of good I've won amid its strife —
   All I have known, that's purely sweet,
Of this old world, or yonder Heaven above —
   I gladly throw them at thy feet,
And crown thee with my love!

www.ingramcontent.com/pod-product-compliance
Lightning Source LLC
Chambersburg PA
CBHW020109170426
43199CB00009B/467